TOM SIMPSON

BIRD ON THE WIRE

Andy McGrath

Foreword by Sir Bradley Wiggins

Rapha.
EDITIONS

For my mother and father,
Margaret and Bob

Rapha.
EDITIONS

British Library Cataloguing-in-Publication Data
A catalogue record for this book is available from the British Library

Library of Congress Cataloguing-in-Publication data has been applied for

2 4 6 8 10 9 7 5 3 1

All images copyright as per credits on page 222

First published in 2017 by Rapha Racing Ltd, Imperial Works, 18 Tileyard, London N7 9AH
rapha.cc

Rapha founder and CEO: Simon Mottram
Publishing director: Daniel Blumire
Design directors: Jack Saunders and
Eve Isaak

Published for Rapha Editions,
in arrangement with
Bluetrain Publishing Ltd
bluetrainpublishing.com

Editor: Guy Andrews
Publishing editor: Taz Darling
Art direction: Bluetrain
Copy editor: Anya Hayes
Image retouching: Linda Duong

Book design: Rob Johnston
robjamesjohnston.com

Printed in Italy by EBS
ISBN 978-1-912164-01-1
All rights reserved

9781472949202

B L O O M S B U R Y

Bloomsbury Sport
An imprint of Bloomsbury Publishing Plc

50 Bedford Square
London
WC1B 3DP
UK

1385 Broadway
New York
NY 10018
USA

bloomsbury.com

BLOOMSBURY and the Diana logo are
trademarks of Bloomsbury Publishing Plc

Bloomsbury Publishing Plc makes every
effort to ensure that the papers used in
the manufacture of our books are natural,
recyclable products made from wood grown
in well-managed forests. Our manufacturing
processes conform to the environmental
regulations of the country of origin.

To find out more about our authors and
books visit bloomsbury.com. Here you will
find extracts, author interviews, details of
forthcoming events and the option to sign
up for our newsletters.

Contents

I first went to the Ghent Six in 1988, when I was eight. I remember seeing the Tom Simpson bust there at the Kuipke velodrome, and my mum telling me the story of who he was and what had happened. I wasn't much bothered about cycling then, and of course I was just a kid. However there was something about it – and about him – that really resonated.

The first time I rode Ghent myself, I used to go to eat each day with Albert Beurick. He was one of those Flemish guys who just needs to be around cycling and cyclists, and he used to run the Café Den Engel. He looked after the Brits who went to try to make a career on the Continent, and he's the guy who seems to pop up in all the photos of Tom. The most famous is the one of the Worlds podium at San Sebastian, with Tom in the rainbow jersey. Albert was his patron, his helping hand and his biggest fan, and he talked to me endlessly and breathlessly about him. I was struck by the depth of feeling he still had for him, and I think that was where it really started for me. I wanted to know Tom, to understand his journey and, I guess, to try to emulate him in some way.

It may seem banal to modern cycling fans, but he became a great champion at a time when British cycling – and as a consequence British *cyclists* – was light years behind the French, the Italian and the Belgians. He played on the whole Englishness thing, and he was obviously extremely patriotic. It was also expedient for him commercially, and both his Englishness and his personality inform his legend. Ultimately though, that whole performance – the tea-drinking, the country gent, the bowler hat – was really just a consequence. None of it would have happened had he not done such extraordinary things on the bike.

I think it's important to contextualise what he did as a rider, because without that you can never truly understand the magnitude of it. The guys he was riding against (and beating) grew up in places like Lombardy, Brittany and Flanders. They were born into an old road racing tradition and emerged as the very best of a large talent pool. Tom Simpson wasn't, and didn't. He was a slight, small, skinny guy who came from a northern English mining village, and yet in 1960 he almost won Paris-Roubaix as a first-year pro.

The following year, at the age of 23, he won the Tour of Flanders. It's indescribably hard to win Flanders in the 21st century, so for him to have done it back then, in that cycling paradigm, almost defies belief. Up against guys like Rik Van Looy and Nino Defilippis, massive engines backed by extremely powerful teams. The system was essentially feudal, and Tom was just starting out. On the bike he looked like a little Spanish climber, so the odds against him being able to win *that* race were colossal. Even today, I still find the fact that he won it almost mystical…

Obviously I never knew him, so to a degree the Tom I know is the one I've imagined into being. Of course it's a romanticised version, and of course his death lends him a celestial quality. That's an essential part of the mystique, just as it is with Fausto Coppi, John Lennon, whoever. That said, it's a fact that Tom shaped the kind of cyclist I aspired to be and later, when I became a professional and a father, the kind of *human being* I aspired to be.

Here was a guy who'd been British pursuit champion, and yet subsequently he went on to win races as diverse as the Tour of Flanders, Tour of Lombardy and Milan-Sanremo. Then he made Ghent his home, wore yellow at the Tour de France and transformed himself into a GC contender. He rode the Sixes and even finished ninth, like me, at Paris–Roubaix.

As a British cyclist, your identity is massively informed by him, so it goes without saying that he was instrumental in my 2012 Tour de France victory. However, one of my abiding memories is climbing Mont Ventoux three years earlier, in 2009. I was fourth overall headed into the stage, a GC entity at last. Tom had been seventh when he died, and somehow I felt worthy of him that day. I rode the stage with a picture of him on my top tube because, that day of all days, I felt particularly close to him.

I still feel close to him, and I think I always will. He gave his life for cycling.

Sir Bradley Wiggins

Introduction

1966 – Tom Simpson:
World Champion

In October 2016, Joanne Simpson made a speech at the unveiling of a 50th anniversary memorial ride for her father in the Belgian cycling mecca, Oudenaarde. "People came up to me and said: 'I never knew your dad won the Tour of Flanders and Milan-San-Remo. I only thought he died on the Ventoux'", she says. "I've got the impression that's the only thing he's remembered for: as the one who died of dope, the first one."

Simpson's death on Mont Ventoux during the 1967 Tour de France, with drugs found in his system, is inextricably, yet excessively, linked to him. Those dark connotations have grown over the rest of his life's story like ivy over a beautiful building. His achievements, rock n' roll racing style and magnetic character made him a popular champion in the first place, his death brought this complicated immortality. Redressing that popular unawareness around his memory is at the very heart of writing this book. There is a lot more lightness and life to Tom Simpson – and new stories to be told.

Simpson was the mine worker's son who went to France with £100 in his pocket and became Britain's first road cycling champion. He took a flurry of ground-breaking wins in the sport's greatest races: the Tour of Flanders, Milan-Sanremo, Bordeaux-Paris, the Tour of Lombardy, Paris-Nice and the World Championships. Small steps for Simpson, giant leaps for cycling kind back home in Britain.

Based in Europe during his career, he was also infused by Continental sport and culture, winning so many hearts as an everyman who mixed intelligence, impulse and ebullience. And just look at him: Simpson had the pull of a matinee idol in cycling's evocative golden age. He has not been done justice photographically until now.

I talked to his close family, friends and fellow former cyclists around the Continent to hear fresh anecdotes and opinions about Simpson. I wanted to explore this multi-dimensional man's personality, his racing successes and his posthumous journey from champion to myth.

Simpson's complex tale and the era in which he raced gripped me too. I'm a romantic, but I didn't want to romanticise anything. As one old racer told me, you don't get to the top by being Mary Poppins; the system didn't allow it. The good and the bad is in here.

It is an especially fitting moment to revisit Tom Simpson's life and times too. As the 50th anniversary of his death on Ventoux and his 80th birthday approach, this is likely the last chance to bring to light new insights from those closest to him.

Seemingly, everyone who crossed his path treasures a fond or funny Tom Simpson story – and even some of those who never met him well up when talking about him. For so many people, the feelings for this great cycling icon are still alive and as strong as ever.

Andy McGrath

10

Chapter One

ONCE IN
A LIFETIME

"Come on, just put your foot down, woman! Get on with it!" Tom Simpson shouted at his wife, Helen, as they hurtled across a railway crossing in northern France on the Lille-Mouscron main road. As ever, he was in a hurry to get back home and she wasn't going fast enough for his liking. It was late July 1965, and Simpson was a broken man with his career in the balance. After abandoning the Tour de France a few days before, in his mad rush to get back from hospital to his house in Ghent, things were about to get much worse.

Their green Mercedes ended up on the wrong side of the road after a railway crossing, as another car approached. The two vehicles skidded and collided. Fruit and beach paraphernalia were strewn across the carriageway from the Dutch holidaymakers they had intercepted. Their front ends were crumpled, but fortunately both parties escaped with no injuries. The Simpsons were not wearing seatbelts – this was before cars were habitually fitted with them – and later discovered that the tyres on the car were almost bald. "It frightened me to death. We could have been killed", Helen says in recollection.

For a man who lived with his foot firmly down on the accelerator, this was another crash in quick succession to go with the exhilarating moments. In the next topsy-turvy 12 months there'd be another car accident, tearful Tour de France abandon and a broken leg sustained while skiing, as well as a dominant victory at the Tour of Lombardy and a Sports Personality of the Year award.

Simpson had quit the Tour de France in tears on the road to Auxerre, just 48 hours before the race's finish. He had bronchitis, blood poisoning and a swollen, badly infected left hand; his body was ruined. But when Tour doctors asked Simpson to quit, he refused. After he finally pulled the plug, he was flown by helicopter to Paris for an emergency operation. Medics told him that if he had waited another day, his affected hand might have required amputation. He spent several days recovering in hospital.

Headline act: at the 1966 Four Days of Dunkirk in France. The race was won by his Peugeot team-mate, Theo Mertens

12

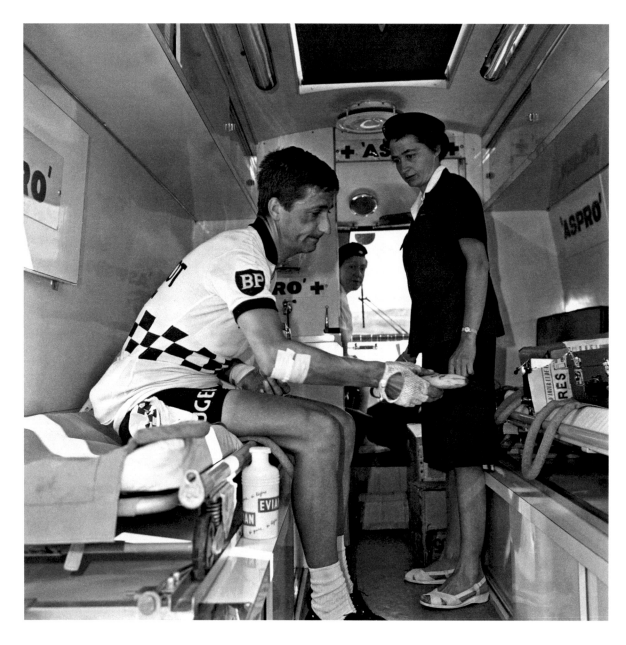

Simpson abandons the race, stage 20, 1965 Tour de France

The British champion had several heart-rending Tour de France abandons during his career, but his 1965 exit was particularly damaging. At the age of 27, he was approaching his physical peak and needed a strong showing there to protect his livelihood. Instead, he failed to win a stage or finish in the top ten, let alone complete the race. In the cut-throat world of Sixties professional cycling, significant earnings were to be made from contracted criterium races around Europe rather than prize money or an annual salary. Invitations for these races were gained based on recent results and publicity. Simpson's last big win was the Milan-Sanremo one-day classic 18 months earlier. In a sport with a short-term memory, his earning power was diminishing and he was running the risk of becoming forgotten – and he knew it. "I'm heartbroken. My season is ruined", he told a journalist at the Tour after quitting into the race ambulance. "I know I will start again though. You always start again. That's your job."

Hope springs eternal, and the World Championships were on the horizon, taking

Shooting the breeze with Jacques Anquetil (right) and Raymond Poulidor (left), 1965

place in early September in the Spanish city of San Sebastian. Organised by the sport's governing body, the Union Cycliste Internationale (UCI), and contested by nations rather than business-backed trade teams, it remains the most prestigious annual event in professional cycling. The winner competes in a rainbow jersey for the following year and is guaranteed lucrative race contracts and endorsements. Simpson knew that this long one-day race had the potential to take him to unprecedented heights. He had come close to triumph a couple of times before, finishing fourth in 1959 and 1964. He told himself that he wouldn't be beaten this time round.

Forced to rest, Simpson couldn't even ride for the first ten days after his injury. The lay-off turned out to be a blessing in disguise, allowing him some precious rest, rare in an era where knackered racers habitually went straight from the Tour de France to cash in on the exhausting criterium circuit for several weeks. It pushed their bank balances into the black and their bodies into the red.

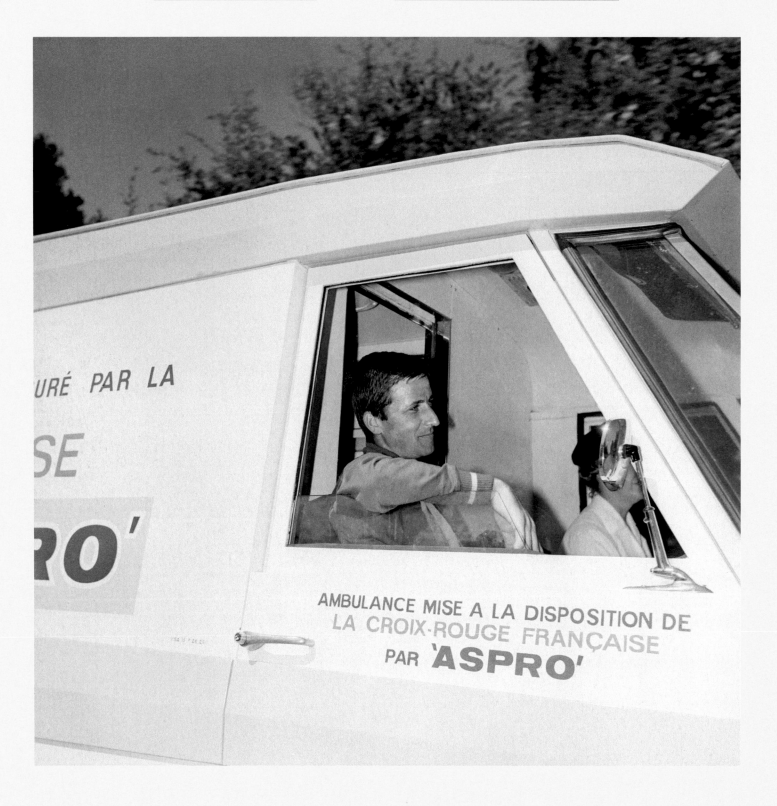

1965 TOUR DE FRANCE: In a reflective
mood after his late abandon

1965 WORLD CHAMPIONSHIPS: The new
world champion in the madding crowd.
Escorted to the podium by Albert Beurick.

Throughout August 1965, Simpson put in hours of training on the spider's web of lanes that criss-cross Belgium, sometimes with compatriot and fellow Ghent-based professional cyclist Vin Denson. "We didn't have any climbs, you had to go quite some distance before you could get into the hills. So we used to concentrate on speed and getting loads of miles in", Denson says. "Tom trained so hard for the World Championships, it was unbelievable. Sometimes, he was lazy; this time, you'd go training and it was a bloody job to come round him. Many times he was so determined, he would win races. I could tell immediately when he wanted to win one. You could look into his eyes and see it." A born competitor, Simpson usually attacked every race with gusto: it literally paid to do so. However, at the final race before the World Championships, the four-day Paris-Luxembourg at the end of August 1965, he decided to help his squad-mates and avoid drawing attention to his good condition.

No rider, however prodigiously talented, can win a top cycling race without the support of a team. They help turn preconceived tactics into reality, protect a leader from the wind, fetch sustenance and offer everything from verbal encouragement to physical pushes. At the World Championships, cohesion is crucial, given the anomalous format of the race, with the sport's best riders in national teams for the only day of the year.

With six starters versus the ten of cycling superpowers Belgium, France and Italy, Great Britain were underdogs. Keith Butler, Vin Denson, Barry Hoban, Alan Ramsbottom and Michael Wright were the determined men selected to support Simpson. It was a tight-knit group: though everyone except Ramsbottom raced for different teams on the Continent during the year, everyone but Wright was based in the Flemish city of Ghent as part of Simpson's gang. Simpson could also count on the help of three more English speakers. "The Australian riders Bill Lawrie, Neville Veale and Bob Patton all lived in Ghent too, and they were also riding for Tom", Keith Butler says. "That was the best of the best."

The squad was fighting meagre means. Cycling was an amateur, Cinderella sport back in Britain, with a modicum of prize money and popular support back home. The British Cycling Federation did not offer a fee, let alone expenses, for its racers, nor did it arrange accommodation or send mechanics and soigneurs: all de rigueur organisational elements of the modern sport. Friends and family members travelling from Belgium acted as team helpers, led by Albert Beurick, whose Ghent-based Café Den Engel was British road racing's spiritual home in the Sixties. Even food for the race was sorted out on the fly: team manager Norman Sheil and Beurick ended up pilfering it from other teams' pits on race day. While the fat Belgian made distracting small talk with other managers, Sheil would grab whatever he could to put in the riders' feed bags.

Travel arrangements were similarly laissez-faire. Simpson had it better than most, driving to San Sebastian over a day and a half in his new BMW with the Australian rider Neville Veale. Barry Hoban bumped into an old acquaintance, Ken Monks, at Paris-Luxembourg and cadged a lift across France in his Ford Zodiac, sleeping in there for the overnight stop.

Meanwhile, team-mate Vin Denson drove down from Ghent with his wife Vi and set up camp on the dramatic cliffs above the Basque city's picture-postcard beaches. He was in good company, alongside *Daily Express* journalist Ron White, Australian racer Bill Lawrie and plenty of spectators. However, they soon discovered that the rain in Spain was straying from the plain. "It was a terrible night, I don't know whether we even slept. Our tent was flattened by the storm, we had to put it in the boot", Denson says. "All these other tents blew into the sea, including Ron White's."

He sought out a hotel room, but "all the spectators had taken them. We were looking around and found a woman who had beds in the attic. She said 'all I've got up there are my fur coats. Use them, and put on the beds anything else you want from the wardrobe.'"

18

Simpson's breakthrough breakaway with André Darrigade, Ab Geldermans and Michele Gismondi, 1959 World Championships in Zandvoort, Holland

The race was based on an undulating 19.1 kilometre circuit around the village of Lasarte-Oria to the south of city. It contained two short hills: one at Urnieta, six kilometres in, and a stiffer ascent at Hernani after 14 kilometres. This was dubbed *Cuesta de la Muerte* (Death Hill): not for its particular difficulty, but due to the fatal accidents that would occasionally happen on this sinuous section of road during its heyday as part of the Spanish Grand Prix in the 1920s and 1930s.

Some parts of the circuit were in a poor state: a French company was hired weeks before the races in a bid to finish off late-running road-works. Conditions were made more treacherous by the constant rain in the days before the race. "It was like monsoons there. Every now and again, a big rock would roll down the hill and land on the road", Denson recalls. "Tom was insistent on going round the circuit three times in training. I said, 'Tom, you're going to get yourself killed with these bloody boulders.' I was absolutely serious, I doubted whether to go out with him. He said 'you're committed now: come on, let's go.' He was so persuasive. You had to follow Tom, he was always the leader."

Those calculated risks paid off. "We knew the course inside out", Denson says. "We'd done so much training around it, by the time the race came, we felt as if it was up there", he adds, tapping the side of his head. "It felt so easy, it was abnormal. I think what we did with Tom is a bit like what Team Sky do, taking Froome and all the climbers to the big mountains [before the race]."

Simpson's meticulous preparation extended to his acquisition of better kit. "The GB jerseys were crap, a funny mixture [of material], they just didn't fit properly", Barry Hoban says. "So, Tom got two made, one for him, one for me." According to him, the pair of wool *maillots* were made by the Milan-based jersey-maker Vittorio Gianni.

All Simpson's hard work flew under the radar: he was hardly mentioned in pre-race dispatches. The favourites were five-time Tour de France winner Jacques Anquetil, one-day star Rik Van Looy, defending world champion Jan Janssen and the Italian rider Gianni Motta.

The World Championship format was a recipe for conflict, as season-long rivals were often brought together under national auspices for one day, while every other prestigious race in the calendar was contested by trade teams. Inter-team arguments, destructive ego trips and acts of collusion have regularly cropped up in the event's long history. Contenders from different nationalities with the same employer might come to an agreement simply to not chase one another's attack down, given the gain for the subsequent twelve months going to the man and his marque.

Second-guessing how rivals would act and exploiting suspected divisions was another advantage. The small, but perfectly-formed Great Britain team was in a position to capitalise on the disarray of several bigger, stronger traditional cycling powers. For instance, France was divided by the self-interest of great rivals Jacques Anquetil and Raymond Poulidor. "If Anquetil wants to ride against Poulidor, nothing

can stop that," said team manager Marcel Bidot.

The Belgian squad was riven by tensions too: Eddy Merckx, at the beginning of his legendary career, was racing his first professional World Championships and had little desire to follow the lead of established number one Rik Van Looy. What's more, team-mate Bernard Van de Kerkchove was transferring to Anquetil's Ford France team in 1966, and there were worries that he might side with the Frenchman.

What Great Britain lacked in manpower and strength-in-depth, they made up for in unity. Simpson committed to paying British team-mates from his own pocket to assure their loyalty, a common incentive at the time. "I'm not telling you how much it was. Quite a lot", Keith Butler says, with a little smile spreading across his features. "Uncle Tom was not un-generous." It was a calculated risk: if Simpson won, he would recoup far more over the following 12 months from race contracts.

Besides, his Great Britain team-mates realised they would find it difficult to challenge

Simpson leads into the finale ahead of eventual winner Jacques Anquetil and Jean Stablinski, 1965 Bordeaux-Paris

20

for a result themselves. "Even if we were in the break, the rest of the crowd would work it over that you couldn't win anyway", Denson says, implying that it was a closed circle at the top of the sport. The difference was that Simpson had forced his way into it and earned respect, having won two of cycling's most respected one-day Classics: the 1961 Tour of Flanders and the 1964 Milan-Sanremo.

Simpson took all three by making it into late breakaways and outsprinting an opponent. His attacking, all-or-nothing approach suited the sport's one-day races, where there were no gains or losses to be taken into account for another day. Simpson may have had the build of a bird, but the heart of a lion.

Yet his words to *Daily Telegraph* journalist David Saunders on the start line in Lasarte suggested a more patient approach. "No more stupid lone efforts for me. I'm going to sit in and wait for my chance – if it comes", Simpson said. The previous year's World Championship

may well have been in his mind. Held around the Alpine town of Sallanches, he had burned precious energy in an impressive 40-mile lone chase to a breakaway. But he still finished an exhausted fourth, 50 metres behind the leaders.

The 1965 World Championship would be a race that favoured the bold. Simpson's team-mate Barry Hoban followed the day's first meaningful move. He correctly predicted that the Spanish team would be racing more with their hearts than their heads, eager to impress on home soil. Lo and behold, when a group of 15 riders – a fifth of the field – broke away on the first lap, there were four Spaniards among them as well as the noted strongmen Peter Post of the Netherlands, Roger Swerts of Belgium, the Italian Franco Balmamion and the Swiss Kurt Bingelli.

After another lap, Simpson instinctively realised it was time to go on the attack. His team-mates Ramsbottom and Denson gave the initial surge, he followed and bridged across to the leaders with the German star Rudi Altig and a fifth Spaniard, Sebastián Elorza.

The group's make-up was ideal. All the dominant nations were represented in front with B-list competitors, save for France, whose rider Joseph Groussard punctured out of the original breakaway. The more fancied team captains were in the bunch behind with little motivation to chase hard: why burn energy pursuing a team-mate? The gap started to grow, along with Simpson's belief, given the arrhythmic pursuit.

Every time he climbed Death Hill, he would hear hearty support in his mother tongue. Four members of the Southport Cycling Club were standing at the top of the climb, having travelled even further than their cycling hero to get there. After taking two weeks' holiday from their respective jobs in Great Britain, they got a berth in a West Indies-bound boat from Southampton, disembarked at its first stop in Vigo and cycled 800 kilometres east to San Sebastian to watch Simpson.

"It rained all day during the race, it was horrible", recalls Ken Beck, one of the quartet. "We kept in the same place trying to stay dry.

On the front page of *Cycling*

SIMPSON IS CHAMP!

Cycling

ONE SHILLING   EVERY WEDNESDAY

TOM'S OWN STORY– EXCLUSIVE

• Italy team trial winners

• Botherel top amateur

• Eicholz bests our girls

A last grimace and Tom Simpson is Britain's first professional champion of the world.

1965 TOUR DE FRANCE: On the attack
on stage one from Cologne to Liège

1965 WORLD CHAMPIONSHIPS: Keeping a
beady eye on Rudi Altig in the finale

"You only get opportunities like this once in a lifetime." Simpson holds off an exhausted Rudi Altig after nearly seven hours of racing, 1965 World Championships

We were stood on this corner and the police wouldn't let us even cross the road, they were right keen."

There were other peculiarities to this World Championships taking place in Franco-era Spain. At all the week's post-race podium presentations, the national anthem of the winner was replaced by the official UCI hymn. One theory is that the dictator, displeased at the presence of the East Germans at the competition, banned their rendition. A few days later, Tom Simpson's occasional track racing partner, the Australian sprinter Ron Baensch, had a brush with Franco's security. The Generalissimo, who used San Sebastian as his summer retreat, was on his way back from church when Baensch and a Dutch rider, Piet van der Touw, returned to their hotel from a training ride ahead of the World Track Championships. Police stopped anyone from crossing the road until Franco had passed. The two cyclists didn't want to wait, tangled with the security and were arrested and beaten.

As the race entered the final 100 kilometres, there were various attacks from contenders such as Sels, Stablinski, Van Looy and Merckx. But they were neutralised by their rivals and the intelligent tactics of Simpson's Great Britain team-mates. They would sit on any attacks, then scupper them by refusing to pull their weight.

Keith Butler recalls following Jacques Anquetil, the great star of the era, as he forced the pace on the front, desperate to bring the gap down. "I thought I was going to die, but I wouldn't let go", he says. Coincidentally, as we dissect the race in his house near Gatwick Airport, the 2016 World Championships are showing on the muted television screen in the background. "You have to do these things. You're riding for a team and a person, you do the job. This is professional bike riding", he says.

If Butler wasn't marking moves, Alan Ramsbottom would be on them in a flash or Vin Denson would be disrupting the chase. "You'd go through and swing off or leave gaps to make people come round you. It was a lot more defensive", Denson says. "You just did nothing and sat on the

back. I think it was ever so good because you've only got to slow them down one or two miles an hour and the breakaway will gain on people."

So it proved. By the start of the eleventh lap, 60 kilometres from the finish, the bunch was eight minutes down and it was game over. The controlling ride from the British boys in blue-and-red had broken their rivals' spirits. Anquetil, Poulidor and Van Looy were among the champions who abandoned the race early.

As the 267-kilometre event approached its finale, the leading group was running out of puff. The Spaniards had tired themselves out and several riders were refusing to work. Simpson was circumspect. "Tom came up to me and asked 'how are you feeling?'" Barry Hoban remembers. "I said 'all right but the legs are starting to twinge a bit.'

He said 'Barry, if you feel like falling off, fall off in front of Franco Balmamion.' Because he was a damn good rider, he won the Giro [twice] without winning a stage. With certain riders, you can tell [from their body language] when they're flying or not; Balmamion was a difficult one to judge."

However, when Simpson and Rudi Altig instigated the winning move with three laps to go on the hill at Hernani, the Italian was nowhere to be seen. The World Championship became an unexpected duel between two stars with points to prove. Simpson's German rival broke his femur at the Tour of Spain that May and was on crutches two months before the race.

Neither could get rid of the other: Simpson later said that he was going stronger on the climbs and that Altig was more powerful on the flats. On the final lap, they stayed together up Death Hill: Altig claimed Simpson had begged him not to attack; Simpson intimated in his autobiography that there was a gentleman's agreement to work together and ride side-by-side from the kilometre to go marker.

Altig had no need to leave his rival behind. Smart money was on the German to win, as a powerful sprinter-roadman who often prevailed in bunch sprints. Simpson was no thoroughbred finisher, but he could maintain his finishing speed well and had saved some energy after six

hours in the lead. Three hundred metres from the line, Simpson launched his sprint as he heard his German rival's chain slip. Altig had made a hash of changing onto his 13 cog, a harder gear. "I don't understand how a great champion of Rudi's class chose to use his derailleur during the sprint. It was a monumental error", Simpson said afterwards. "You only get opportunities like that once in a lifetime, and I jumped at it."

Unable to get back on terms, Altig stopped pedalling in the final 25 metres. Simpson crossed the line several lengths ahead, his cropped brown hair flattened by the rain, his head thrown back and his mouth agape in a huge smile. Then, mayhem. Britain's first elite men's world champion was engulfed by a throng of fans, spectators, policemen and pressmen. His biggest supporter, Albert Beurick, picked him up, bike and all, unaware of his own strength. Peugeot directeur sportif Gaston Plaud plonked a liveried casquette on his head to ensure that the brand would get more coverage. *Cycling* editor Alan Gayfer vaulted over a seven-foot wall into a gutter to get near to the new champion.

"Today, I was Cassius Clay", Simpson, often a man for a good quote, told journalists. "This was an easy race for me, really easy. It was not that I disregarded the others, or believed that the race was not important, but I never felt in better condition than when I started this championship. We British professionals had decided that we had had enough of losing championships and this time, we were all working together."

Hoban trailed in behind the breakaway and Ramsbottom finished with the remnants of the bunch. The usually reserved Lancastrian gave Simpson an inkling of his victory's significance, kissing him on both cheeks, Continental style. The rest of the British team found out about his victory from a group of press motorcycle drivers alongside them, providing a running commentary. "When they said he was with Altig, we thought 'Oh Christ, not him.' We were determined he was going to get second", Denson recalls.

Simpson could go from the sublime to the ridiculous in a heartbeat. Rushing off afterwards

Portrait of a champion on the cover of *Sporting Cyclist* by Glenn Steward. Steward was art editor of Jock Wadley's magazine and a keen cyclist himself

to Biarritz to catch a specially chartered flight to the Circuit de l'Aulne in Brittany, a lucrative criterium the following day, Simpson left behind his new rainbow jersey and bag, containing his medal. He had to borrow kit from the outgoing champion Jan Janssen and a pair of shorts from Raymond Poulidor for the race.

His team-mates shared a quick glass of champagne with Simpson, and set off on the long drive back to Belgium the following day. On the face of things, it was business as usual. But, just weeks after Bob Dylan went electric at Newport, a similar charge swept through the sport at San Sebastian. The subsequent editorial in the pages of *Cycling* emphasised the turning point: "We have waited 33 years for this moment, for the time when we could hold up our heads in world racing and say 'There goes a Briton, Champion of the World in the professional game.' This is the hardest side of the sport, and a young miner's son from Durham has proved that anything a Belgian or a Frenchman can do, we can do just as well."

Achieved at a time when British cycling had next to no organisation or elite success on the road and a numerical disadvantage at the race itself, the quality of his win has only appreciated with time. "It was fantastic", Keith Butler says. "I still get a little shiver thinking about it now: bloody hell, we did it."

Simpson's victory altered the perception of British cyclists on the Continent. "It really made the world see that Britain were among the leading contenders in the world of cycling. Right through the Sixties, we had this respect", Vin Denson says. The following year, he became Britain's first Giro stage winner, while super sprinter Barry Hoban went on to win eight Tour stages.

The rainbow jersey relaunched Simpson's career and ensured his greatest fame and popularity back home and on the Continent. It summed up his spirit: when you're down, keep attacking. Here was a tightrope walker of fate, an irrepressible risk taker who had swung dramatically from a hospital bed and car crash to the top of the world, a sportsman to grip the public like no other.

30

Chapter Two

SHIT OR BUST

SIMPSON

On a rainy September morning, Sky TV is on in the deserted bar area of Harworth and Bircotes Sports Pavilion. The parking bays outside are empty, and wooden chairs are stacked on the dozen adjacent tables.

Tom Simpson never stayed in one place for long during his life, but it was here, in this colliery town of red-brick terraced houses, that he became a man and a racing cyclist. As Julie the barwoman goes back and forth to the metal tea urn in the corner, she chats about how Harworth's most famous son died. Behind her, in the backroom, there are rolls of honour for the village football team, Harworth Colliery FC. Signed shirts by the former Manchester United player Norman Whiteside and the Doncaster Rovers team take pride of place on the walls. Between the two rooms, it would be easy to miss a large, glass-fronted wooden case in the corridor: the Tom Simpson Museum.

"It's not a museum, just a cabinet", Julie says, as she brings over a cup of builder's tea. This tribute is festooned with memorabilia from his career: press clippings, photographs, a replica Peugeot bicycle and his racing jersey, complete with race number, from the 1967 Tour de France. Cyclists and fans visit from around the world; there are best wishes in the guestbook from New Zealand and Australia.

Simpson's old friend and cycling clubmate Len Jones meets me here. He has the appearance and energy of a man far younger than his 76 years, often preceding a recollection with a "Hey!" before recounting it, as if it's just struck him. Living here since he was a toddler, Jones has seen the rise and decline of Harworth. He points out of the pavilion's backroom window to a cluster of trees: until its demolition in April 2016, a decade after the colliery's closure, a 78-metre pit head tower stood there, bestriding the horizon and characterising this proud mining community. Generations of townspeople would either go down the pit or work at the prosperous shoe or lightbulb factories. For lads from these parts, full-time professional cyclist was about as plausible a profession as astronaut or King of England.

Jones and Simpson were training partners and young members of the Harworth and District Cycling Club in the early 1950s. When they first tagged onto club runs as raw children, it was a case of putting up, shutting up and trying to keep up with their fitter elders on 90-mile rides. "I can remember once when we were coming back from Market Rasen one winter. Tom and I were absolutely shattered. My brother and some older riders used to put their hands on our backs and push us", Jones says. "Sometimes I were bloody dropping to sleep. It started snowing and you got wet and cold. We were just wearing wool, shorts and long stockings, corduroy trousers with clips if it were really cold, leather cycling shoes, two or three pairs of socks. But it made us hard as nails when we got older."

Classic sibling competitiveness first spurred Simpson to join the local club with his older brother, Harry. He got a taste for the sport from maiden races haring round the block on his brother-in-law's thick-tyred heffer of a bicycle, trying to beat his mates' times.

On that same cumbersome steed, the 13-year-old Simpson stopped the clock at 17 minutes 50 seconds over five miles in his maiden time-trial: nothing to give incumbent cycling star Louison Bobet sleepless nights. To save for a proper racing bicycle, Simpson got a weekend job delivering bread and groceries on a basket-laden bike. After months of pestering a colliery man who lived on his round, he traded it for a lighter version. As Simpson gave his modest salary to his parents – the family was living just above the breadline – it was a case of patiently accumulating pocket money to buy bits and bobs. Eventually, he had a passable hotchpotch of a machine.

A late developer, there was no immediate inkling that the adolescent Simpson would become "the village lad who reached the top of the tree in world cycling", as a local speech-maker later dubbed him. Sometimes, he would be dropped on the hills of the club run and reach

At home in Ghent, 1966

the assigned tea stop as the older riders were starting back, following their break, giving him no rest. His clubmates playfully anointed him "Four-Stone Coppi" after Fausto, the Italian champion, who had a similarly skinny build and prominent nose. Simpson liked being compared to a hero who featured in his compiled cycling scrapbooks of stars.

"He used to say 'I'm dreaming of them and I'm going to be one before I'm finished'", his mother Alice told filmmaker Ray Pascoe in 1968. "I never thought he would accomplish it." As Simpson improved, he had a fight on his hands to be the star of Harworth and District CC, let alone the region. Though two-and-a-half years younger, his friend Len Jones was precocious and often ran him close.

"Second were no good to Tom", Jones says. "It were like coming last. He had to win. If I rode a time-trial and beat him with more of a gap than normal, he wouldn't train with me and the lads for two weeks. He ignored me. Tom would be out training on his own. If we came the other way, he'd turn left, or turn round and go back. Just to avoid us."

After those years off the back, the prodigious teenagers were routinely handing out beatings to their elders – and Simpson let them know it. After winning the club 25-mile time-trial with a mark just over the hour, the 15-year-old went round the clubroom bragging about his victory, to a sour reaction. "Little stars don't shine bright for long", one wag told him.

"He were cocky in some ways, a bit sarcastic. It used to put people off", Jones says. "My missus used to sense it, she didn't like him at all. She said, 'he uses you, he don't show you no respect.'"

The climb of Moscar is long and steady, heading west out of the industrial Yorkshire city of Sheffield. Framed by stone walls and with scant vegetation, it is a mere canapé before the more fulfilling climbs and panoramas further along the Peak District ridge road at Ladybower Reservoir and Snake Pass.

One day in 1954, Pete Ryalls was riding up the hill with a friend on his four-speed bike when he spotted a pair of fellow cyclists in the distance. So much has changed since then – gearings and traffic counts, for one. Back then on this tourist-friendly route, you could ride for hours without seeing a car. But one thing remains the same: the cyclist's innate competitive urge upon turning a bend and seeing someone else pedalling. Young or old, on sit-up-and-beg or space-age carbon frame, it puts immediate wind in one's sails. It might be insignificant, but chasing and passing a stranger goes right down to simplistic mano-a-mano instinct too. In a matter of moments, you assess whether the prey is fair game, nearing or pulling away.

As one of the best junior racers in South Yorkshire, Ryalls was approaching fast and had one thing in mind. "We thought 'let's see what we can do with these two'", he says. "We reckoned we were the bee's knees. I'm afraid it didn't take us long to find that there was no way we were going to get rid of them. That was my first meeting with Tom Simpson, before I knew him at all. The strength was there."

Ryalls soon got a taste of the competitive punishment that his fellow 17-year-old could mete out at a June 1955 race around the Doncaster village of Sprotbrough. "It didn't take you long

With his mother Alice outside the Simpson house in Harworth. Hats were a regular Simpson comedy prop, 1956

Tea time in the Simpson household and it's pies all round

Ryalls recalls the Burbage Junior Road Race in 1955, a 48-mile junior event which centred around the Peak District moor. As usual, Simpson set a fierce pace and whittled the group down to six leaders before that final climb. He had a spare tubular tyre slung around his neck, mimicking his Continental cycling heroes, and his left elbow was bandaged from his latest fall. "Tom was crash-prone because he was impetuous", Ryalls adds.

Ryalls dropped back on Burbage Moor, reeling in a few others at his own pace. "Eventually, I caught Tom. It was the last bit of a climb before we descended to the finish. And he was in tears, walking. He had completely blown. It's just another example of what I'm talking about. He could drive himself into the ground – and let's face it, that's what he did in the end."

The young Simpson stood out for more than his erratic racing style: hailing from the rural community of Haswell in County Durham, a hundred miles to the north, his softer burr distinguished him from the regional crowd. Simpson was born there on November 30 1937, the youngest of six to Alice and Tom Senior, a conveyor worker in the local mine.

Initially, the family made a little go a long way, sharing a house with two bedrooms, a living room and a pantry, before moving to larger lodgings above the working men's club, which his parents took charge of. World War Two rationing made for slim pickings throughout his childhood. While air raid sirens went off regularly, Haswell was virtually untouched by the fighting. In its only raid, German aircraft dropped sticky bombs on the nearby Northern Sabulite explosive works; they missed, and the only casualties were a pair of cows in the nearby fields.

Once the Simpsons moved to the bustling mining community of Harworth in 1950, Tom struck upon a much richer seam of cycling interest. There was a variety of clubs in the Doncaster and Sheffield area, and cycle racing on shale or grass tracks was a staple of the local miners' welfare sports meetings, dotted around the South Yorkshire coalfield through the year.

to find out that you were up against something special because you couldn't get him off the front. That's the first thing I noticed: when is this guy going to stop? He needs a rest. People with big engines tend to do that rather than giving short stabs. There was no way he would let the pace drop, and that's what got to everybody."

As the race entered its final lap, only Ryalls was still with Simpson, hanging on desperately. The last time up the hill at High Melton, just before the finish, the stronger man cut him loose and won by 17 seconds. "There was nothing that changed from there, as far as I could see that made him anything other than pretty bloody exceptional", Ryalls says.

"In 1955, we were both in our final years as juniors and we were the top two in the division. Over that season, I suppose I got over the line first more often than he did. But when he won a race, when he decided to take off, I wasn't in the same league. Basically, he would win the race or finish nowhere. That was Tom: I described him as 'shit or bust Simpson'."

"I don't think he could actually control himself, particularly in the younger days. Obviously as he became a top-class pro, he had to calm it down a bit. But if you look through the results and look back at the way he rode, it was really just the same. You never saw him away from the front."

However, Great Britain was light years behind the established European nations of cycling. Simpson's club belonged to the National Cycling Union (NCU), an organisation that did not permit racing on open roads, for fear that the police would subsequently prohibit all cycling. Their bitter rivals were the arriviste breakaway body, the British League of Racing Cyclists (BLRC), which sprung up during World War Two. They waged a contemptuous civil war that divided British cyclists. Being a "Leaguer" or a "Unionist" gave members a

tribe and a profoundly different experience of competitive cycling.

The traditionalist NCU preferred dark, incongruous clothing, track racing and a fixed gear: when junior rival Pete Ryalls first met Simpson on the climb of Moscar, he could immediately tell this stranger's allegiance from his saddle bag and single sprocket, the hallmarks of an NCU affiliate. BLRC members raced on the highways, used derailleurs and favoured Continental-style club names and clothing. They were the ones who ultimately pushed through

Deep in conversation with friends during a break from riding

road racing in Britain. In 1951, they organised a Tour of Britain race – Simpson played truant from school one day to see a stage finish in Nottingham – and received intermittent invitations to Continental races like the Peace Race, a gruelling, fortnight-long event through Eastern Europe, paved the way for a first British team at the Tour de France in 1955. Until then, British cyclists rarely raced outside of their own country.

Eligible for junior races on his 16th birthday, Simpson was keen to race on the open highway too. He knew he would never be in the firmament alongside heroes like Coppi and Ferdi Kübler if restricted to the NCU beat of track and time-trials.

Simpson proposed BLRC membership at the Harworth and District club annual general meeting in 1953, with Len Jones as seconder. Their clubmates refused to even entertain the thought. "Eventually I sat down and said 'you might as well too Tom, it's a waste of time.' But no, he wanted it voted on", Jones recalls. "It must have been going on for 30 minutes. In the end, the meeting didn't end properly: they all got up and walked out, leaving me and Tom on our own." The anecdote

All smiles with friends Tony Hart, Marlene Shaw and George Shaw (left to right) at the Monsal hill climb, 1956. Simpson won it the following year

shows his determination and confidence: Simpson thought nothing of challenging his elders.

If you can't convert 'em, join 'em: Simpson left for BLRC club Scala Wheelers of Rotherham, setting up his own road racing sub-team with Mick Bingham, Maurice Hart and, later, George Shaw. Hart recalls a young man with an individualistic streak: "Tom was so mad keen, he didn't want to ride as a team as much as he wanted to go off the front and disappear down the road."

Scala support did, however, come to his rescue at a 1956 race around the Chesterfield village of Whittington. Simpson suffered a front wheel puncture, the trio of team-mates stopped together and Hart used his brand new CO_2 cartridge to reinflate the tyre, before chasing back on together. "When we caught the bunch, it was at the bottom of the steep Whittington hill", Hart says. "Mick and I went 'Thank God for that', and slipped in with the other riders. Tom didn't. The last I saw of him was rounding the outside of the bunch and disappearing over the hill's brow. He went on to win the race."

The BLRC took much inspiration from

Joking around with Joan "The Body" Johnson at Walt's Café, Blyth, 1956

top-level European racing, which Simpson and company had seen in cycling magazines. Hart remembers a 1956 race in the Derbyshire lanes when "Four-Stone Coppi" was the butt of a few jokes for racing in a Swiss jersey, adorned with red background and a white cross rather than his usual Scala blue. But in many ways, his peers were the pretenders paying lip service to the sport's heroes and heartland; Simpson was the one who was dead serious about emulating them. They probably weren't laughing at Simpson any more after he rode off and triumphed that day.

During his teenage years, Simpson's thirst for self-improvement led him to regularly exchanging letters with several experienced elders. One such was George Berger, a naturalised Austrian who had raced in France as an amateur. Berger advised the young man to take up track pursuiting, to give him a smooth cadence and an engine for road racing.

The other great influence on his fledgling career was Cyril Cartwright, a Manchester-based

Simpson and the gang, 1956

miner who broke the national 25-mile record, a significant milestone in time-trialling. Simpson spent two weeks *chez Cartwright* before the 1956 national amateur 4,000-metre pursuit championship, the first of several stay-overs there. The former champion lent him his own track bicycle, improved his riding position and developed his racing craft. Soon, Cartwright had imparted a career's worth of wisdom.

He impressed the importance of eating healthily on him too: on his return to Harworth, Simpson badgered his mother for salad and fresh fruit galore, instead of regular fare like chips or gravy and mash – not easy or cheap to acquire in a Nottinghamshire colliery town. This fixation with healthy food stayed with him throughout his career.

"There was lettuce, sultanas, mixed nuts, grated carrot, sliced bananas, grapes, sliced apple, pear. And when he ate it, I says, you know how much that plate of salad cost me today, boy?" his mother Alice told Ray Pascoe in 1968.

This was just one facet of his teenage self-discipline. Sometimes, after working as an apprentice draughtsman in Retford, he would train in the evenings. Then, while his parents watched television at 9pm, he would be in his dressing gown and ready for bed. Even then, Simpson appreciated such sacrifice was a means to an end. "I says to him 'you lead a life like a monk sometimes, boy'", Alice Simpson recalled to Ray Pascoe. "And he says, 'I wanted to pay myself back. I'm not working hard for nothing.'"

With Cartwright's help, Simpson came from nowhere to nearly win the 1956 pursuit title. On the way to second place, he beat the amateur world pursuit champion Norman Sheil in qualifying. It was the catalyst which took him to the cusp of the national team. Little over a year after trudging up Burbage Moor in tears, Simpson was picked for the Olympic Games team pursuit in Melbourne.

First, there were preparatory meets in Russia and Eastern Europe. His darting speed and featherweight frame earned him the nickname of

"The Sparrow" out there. Away from the racing, it was eventful too: Simpson fell asleep at the Bolshoi ballet and was put under house arrest on the Romania border with the rest of the team for failing to have the correct paperwork. Simpson's dedication to the cause was clear: he accepted an invitation to stay for an extra week of racing that meant he missed his brother's wedding back home.

At the Olympics, the baby of the track team roomed with the road race squad's equivalent, a draughtsman from Hull called Billy Holmes. Arriving weeks before the races and unaccustomed to the quantity and rigour of training, both greenhorns were left demoralised. "I rode through Melbourne back to the Olympic village so depressed", Holmes says. "Thinking if I can't train with these guys, how can I race? I thought I would talk to Tommy about it. I go in the room, hang my bike up and Tommy's got his head in his hands. He's crying."

"'I can't do it, Billy,' he says. 'They'll have to send me home. I can't do these half laps. I can't keep the rhythm, I can't do it.'"

They confided their doubts to team manager Benny Foster. A paraffin salesman when not at the helm of the British cycling team, Foster was a firm believer in Simpson's ability, but likened the prodigy to unstable dynamite. His explosive mix of supreme confidence, abundant energy and over-exuberance could be a help and a hindrance. During their Olympic semi-final against Italy, he detonated too soon. Simpson pulled an overly long turn, failed to latch onto the rear of the line after swinging off and was dropped. Though Great Britain later beat South Africa for the bronze medal, Simpson felt personally responsible for wrecking the team's chances of winning gold. He worked himself into such a state over this error that he wept after later watching British athlete Chris Brasher win the 5,000 metres in the Olympic stadium, feeling the result had partly atoned for his own error.

While those incidents were serious, everything around the racing sounds like it

Simpson and the Hart brothers at Walt's Cafe, Blyth, fresh from a long bank holiday ride in the Derbyshire hills, 1956

40

Riding out through the
North London suburbs
in the early morning
with Billy Holmes, 1965
London to Holyhead

belongs in a *Carry On* film. A joker who wore a permanent smile, Simpson had found kindred spirits in the likes of Holmes, pursuit team-mate John Geddes and track sprinter Eric Thompson. There was mischief at the opening ceremony, where they punched their team-issue hats into bowlers for a laugh. Water fights helped to take the edge off the Melbourne heat, they shinned up lampposts to spy on the separate women's quarters and had a pillow fight with the Great Britain wrestlers on the flight home.

The pick of the pranking was when the cycling team decided to steal the Olympic flag at the entrance of the village. "It was as big as that wall", Holmes recalls, pointing in his spacious living room. "The flag pole had armed guards around it." While he distracted them with a tall tale, Thompson shinned up with a hacksaw. "Simpy would have been in the mix of it all. Then we stitched it into Geddes's mattress, under his bed. The chef de mission put bloody hell on the next day. There was security everywhere, asking who had pinched it. We had to give it back, but we said we wanted a proper handing over ceremony. They didn't like that. Our team manager Benny Foster went absolutely mad, but he was thrilled too because we got medals. Winning cycling medals at Olympic Games in them days weren't like it is now", Holmes, who returned with a team road race silver medal, says.

Back home, Simpson was still one of the lads. Maurice Hart remembers going to a friend's house after a dance in Rotherham that winter: "We walked into the little dining room and Tom was sat on a settee with a girl on each arm, showing them his bronze medal."

"Oh yes, he was popular with the ladies", he says. "I took a picture of Tom cuddling up to a girl called Joan. We used to call her 'The Body', she frequented the wooden hut we all went to after racing. Tom is laid with his head back, laughing and joking. I treasure that because it's him down to a tee, larking about; he was a bit of a comedian. We'd go to Walt's Café [the Blyth-based hub for south Yorkshire cyclists

back then], take it in turns to chat Joan up and, if we could, take her outside for ten minutes for a good snog. Everyone used to cheer when you walked back in."

Simpson could still be similarly laidback with his racing too: one day, he'd beat all-comers, the next he wouldn't turn up, sometimes literally. In mid-April 1957, he won the 1,000 metres and Devil take the hindmost on the local Brodsworth track. The next morning, he arrived late for the start of the Stocksbridge Coureurs 55-mile road race. He put his head down and chased the pack, but it was a hopeless cause. You could expect the unexpected with Simpson.

He joined the respected Fallowfield Club in April 1957, set up by British sprint cycling great Reg Harris. Over the next two seasons, Simpson established himself as a consistent contender in national track events, winning the Daily Herald Gold Trophy in Manchester and the Good Friday omnium at Herne Hill. The discipline also helped to give him leg speed and an enduring, fluid pedalling style. In later years, there was poetry to Simpson in motion: with his straight back and long legs, he made many all-out efforts appear insouciant.

His fragile build disguised his power and drive. Before the 1958 Empire Games, a medical research team at St Athans RAF station took radiographs and other physical data from the team. According to manager Benny Foster, when it came to Simpson's turn, they laughed at his appearance and asked if he came from Belsen. Amusement turned to surprise when this apparent weakling's sublime results emerged.

In the racing at the nearby Maindy track, Simpson was pipped to pursuit gold by his domestic *bête noire* Norman Sheil. It was so close that for years afterwards, Simpson, rarely the best loser, still reckoned he had beaten the Liverpudlian. It was a disappointment to go alongside several others: crashes at the world pursuit championship in 1957 and 1958 also robbed him of the chance to make a bigger name for himself.

Team pursuit training at the Olympics: (front to back) Alan Danson, Simpson, John Geddes and Donald Burgess, 1956

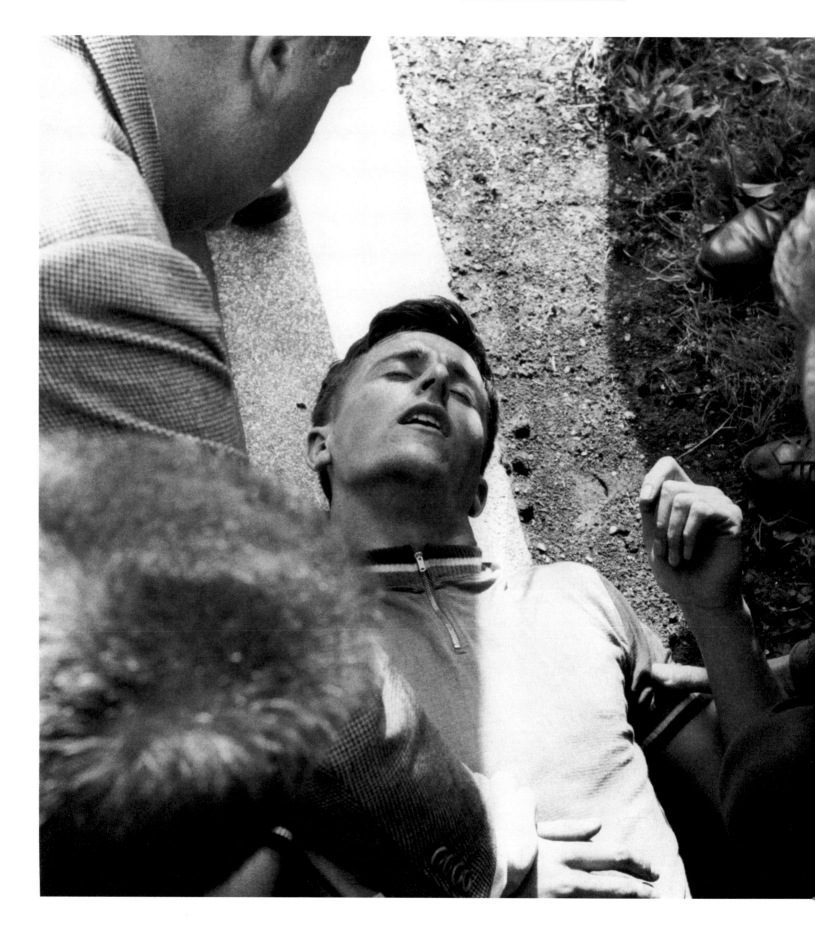

Simpson crashes after finishing his first round effort against defending champion Carlo Simonigh. He suffered concussion and a broken jaw, but having qualified for the next round, still raced the subsequent quarter-final, 1958 Amateur World Track Championships, Paris

Nevertheless, Simpson saw himself as a world-beater, and set out to prove it to everyone else by toppling the amateur hour record in November 1958 in Zurich. He wanted it to be the grand opener to a successful European trip that would catch the eye of promoters and teams on the Continent. First, he needed to take yet more leave from work. In between his occasional European sojourns, Simpson was a full-time draughtsman, having moved to the Glass Bulbs factory in Harworth. His understanding supervisor, Mr Cowhig, permitted him more time off and said that he would still have his job if he returned, but if his efforts failed, that would be the end of the gallivanting. Helped by a winning charm and thousand-volt smile, Simpson could often push the boundaries of acceptability and still emerge as endearing, whether it be getting excessive time off from his employers, spending weeks at Cyril Cartwright's house or giving his doting mother culinary complications.

His bid to rock Europe failed. He couldn't hold the required pace in the second half of his hour record bid and finished with 43.804 kilometres, just over a mile short of the mark set by the Swiss Fredy Rüegg a fortnight earlier. The freezing conditions also gave Simpson considerable eye pain, and he ended up spending his 21st birthday in bed, recovering.

Soon afterwards, he travelled to race in Ghent, with verbal contracts for track events at Brussels and Antwerp arranged for afterwards. Those were annulled after he lapped the field twice in the Sportpaleis, giving the local favourites a hiding. Simpson's puppyish energy and fierce desire to win let him down again; sharing pieces of the proverbial pie with peers would have been shrewder for future favour and his finances. Reflecting in mid-1967 on what he learned from that period to help him, he said: "Nothing, I was too stupid to learn then."

But disheartened? Never: he still reckoned Europe was the place for him. A certain amount of naivety and blissful ignorance alongside this

Escape to victory
at the Swanwick
Road Race near
Chesterfield, 1956

steadfast self-belief perhaps helped, considering the world he hoped to conquer existed to Simpson in abstract form, principally an amalgamation from collected wisdom and his magazines. The only available precedent was that of Brian Robinson, a Yorkshireman who was Britain's first Tour de France finisher in 1955, and a stage winner three years later. He lived like a Frenchman, raced on a French team and occasionally beat them at their own game.

Although only 21 years old, Simpson felt that he had experienced the limits of what the British scene could offer. There were no more fearsome rivals to use as yardsticks and there was precious little money to be made – although with Simpson, the Bob Dylan line "when you ain't got nothing, you got nothing to lose" springs to mind. He wrote to Robert and Yvon Murphy, two Breton brothers with Irish lineage whom he had met while racing at Fallowfield. They agreed to house him in April 1959 in the town of Saint-Brieuc in northwest France.

A dampener on his dream was rapidly approaching: compulsory two-year national service. An RAF medical at the start of 1959 meant a call-up was nigh. While peers like Ryalls, Alan Ramsbottom and Vin Denson, all future Tour de France team-mates of his, dutifully went through conscription, Simpson marched to his own beat, not that of any army drill sergeant. He had the courage to follow his instincts, despite the faint dishonour attached to perceived draft dodgers and the disagreement of his father.

"At first, I was against it because national service was on at the time", Tom Simpson Senior told filmmaker Ray Pascoe in 1968. "He says to me, 'Dad, I don't want to be sitting here in 20 years' time, saying to myself 'I wonder where I would have been if I'd went to France?' I said fair enough, lad." Simpson departed for Brittany and an unknown world on April 1 1959, with £100 in his pocket. It was probably the best-timed breakaway of his whole career: his RAF call-up papers arrived in the post the next day.

50

Chapter Three

THE CRAZY ENGLISHMAN

Fresh-faced and bright-eyed ahead of the opening stage of his debut Tour de France, Lille, 1960

"In this world of ours, the sparrow must live like a hawk if he is to fly at all"

Hayao Miyazaki, animator and author

The slag heaps rise on the horizon like ebony pyramids. Every now and then, a towering pithead appears, standing over the landscape like a metal sentinel. Through a cacophony of horns from following cars and motorbikes, one man leads. He wears a long-sleeved Rapha-Gitane top with a yellow top section, a white midriff and a grey lower third. The peak of his white casquette is turned up; the roads are a little damp, but his face and legs are spotless. Alone in front on the cobblestones of northern France, the debutant Tom Simpson is 20 kilometres away from winning Paris-Roubaix.

He turns to Jean Bobet, the *L'Equipe* journalist following on a motorcycle, and asks "how much further?" That's when they know that the end of his breakaway is nigh: the question shows his doubt and fatigue. His pursuers, Pino Cerami and Tino Sabbadini, come barrelling past him on the race's last difficult cobbled sector, 5 kilometres from the finish. If only he had known he was so close to the end. So near, so far: Simpson ended up ninth, yet deemed the moral victor by the media.

There's winning ugly and losing beautifully, and then there's losing beautifully in front of a bumper audience. The Continental television channel Eurovision was broadcasting the race live for the first time. It meant prime screen time for Simpson and the airing of his underdog drama to a giant viewership. "Simpson offered us one of the purest cycling images that we have ever seen: of a young man with still, straight shoulders, but legs in harmony, of a perfectly balanced athlete gifted with the essential qualities that make great champions: fight and ambition", Jean Bobet wrote afterwards.

The 1960 Paris-Roubaix was Simpson's first examination on the cobbles of the North, yet he rode like he belonged there. His initial acceleration on the drag at Moncheaux, 45 kilometres from the finish, stunned his rivals. "Simpson went like a meteor", French rival René Privat told the press afterwards.

Like art or music, sport is an innate expression of personality too. The football pitch or open road is a place for expressing one's hope or disillusion, happiness or anger, flair or reserve, fight or flight mechanisms. Simpson's move at Paris-Roubaix characterised him as a man with a seemingly bottomless reservoir of courage, who makes something happen rather than waiting, as his impetuous move to France in April 1959 had shown.

Simpson was an oddity in this world. Embedding himself in Saint-Brieuc from the colliery town of Harworth, he might as well have been from Mars for all that it meant in Continental cycling circles. On arrival at the coastal Breton town, the Murphy family with whom he was staying did their best to welcome Simpson, but possessing little more French than *oui* and *non*, it was inevitably a lonely environment. "I am a naturally talkative chap and the inability to converse with anybody, even just remarking about the weather or things like that, made me very glum", Simpson wrote in his autobiography, *Cycling is My Life*.

That typically British crutch of conversation would have come up too: jutting out into the Atlantic in France's north-west, Brittany is a land characterised by wet and windy weather. Culturally, it is known for its distinctive *galette* pancakes and cider: an old French joke has it that they guzzle twice as much alcohol here as the rest of the country.

In this distant corner, they also possess a deep intoxication for cycling. Simpson was accustomed to racing at weekends in Britain; here, he could compete in several races a week. The little villages dotted around the countryside regularly closed down for *pardons*, the region's Catholic festivals of penitence, dating back to the 15th century. These involved a mass, a short walk with the church's local saint, crosses and colourful banners, a meal and, sometimes, a cycle race on a short, sharp circuit.

The Breton school of hard knocks has some lofty alumni, including Tour de France winners Lucien Petit-Breton, Jean Robic, Louison Bobet and Bernard Hinault, who joined Simpson's first French club, the Olympique Briochin, 12 years after the Briton.

It wasn't easy to break into this competitive scene as a foreigner, as combines between local riders were a regular obstacle. Even the partisan crowd could get involved; at one race in Châteaulin, Spanish great Federico Bahamontes was whacked with a plank of wood by a spectator, infuriated that he had beaten a local rider for a sizeable prime, which is a mid-race sprint for prize money.

Then there was the language barrier. During his first months of racing, Simpson had to ask fellow riders when the final lap was before he could let his legs do the rest of the talking.

Breaking away late at Paris-Roubaix to gain some valuable airtime as the cobbled classic is televised live for the first time, 1960

Brian Robinson and Simpson messing around, 1960

Simpson wasn't the only *Saoz* in Saint-Brieuc. The Murphys informed him of the presence of a young woman called Helen Sherburn, working down the road as an au pair. One day, Simpson excitably went to knock on her door before shyness got the better of him. Unable to think of what to say, he ran off without meeting her.

When the news reached Sherburn, she walked by the Murphys' house on the way back from dropping the children off at nursery and spotted a sunglasses-clad, Continental-looking fellow, reclining in the garden. Asking in flawless French whether this was where the Englishman lived, Simpson mistook her for another prying local. "Bugger off!" he said.

Once the initial confusion was cleared, he was delighted to chat freely to someone in English. There was the added serendipity that, coming from Askern on the outskirts of Doncaster, she was from his neck of the woods. Helen liked him, but felt that Simpson only had eyes for cycling. It wasn't until the end of the season that he made his affections clearer.

A stage win at the four-day Essor Breton helped to earn him selection into the VC XII team for the Route de France in mid-June 1959. The eight-stage race was effectively the amateur Tour de France. As the only foreigner in a field of talented Frenchmen, Simpson was an exotic creature. "One evening while eating dinner, we said 'fuck, there's an Englishman there'", recalls Henri Duez, who won the race and went on to become Simpson's team-mate at Peugeot. "He attacked every day; he didn't have too much confidence in himself then, it was his debut. But every day, we saw something more from him."

Simpson adapted quickly to the higher pace and distance of stages, but was unsurprisingly ill at ease when the race hit the Pyrenees. The climbs of the Tourmalet and Aubisque were another level compared to Mam Tor and his familiar Peak District molehills. For several days, Simpson toyed with the shame of not being able to finish the longest race of his life; throughout his Breton sojourn, this fear of failure, of returning

Though he won his second race in Brittany, Simpson was overly generous with his efforts during his six months there. His rawness and hunger led to basic mistakes. Twelve months to the day before his Paris-Roubaix revelation, he rolled his tubular tyre off on the first corner of a Breton village race after gluing it incorrectly. At a race in Plougonver, he wrecked his chances of taking the £90 first prize by going for £5 primes during the race and running out of steam prematurely. "I am as strong as anybody in Brittany. All I need now is a head. I throw away too much energy", Simpson told the British journalist Jock Wadley. In spite of this, Simpson still won four races by the end of his first month.

Word quickly spread around Saint-Brieuc about the lesser-spotted *Saoz* – Breton for English person – who was staying with the local butchers. He was a novelty, in the same way a chap from north-western France pitching up at a small village in Yorkshire and smashing centuries at their local cricket club would be.

to Harworth with an empty wallet and dream, was driving him on.

Then, on the last stage, something switched. He glimpsed a signpost for the finish town of Hossegor and, emboldened by the knowledge he would make it, broke away with French rider François Le Bihan and outsprinted him for the stage win.

With this boost to his confidence, Simpson headed to the World Championships in the Netherlands, looking to win both the individual pursuit and the professional road race. It was a sign of his versatility that he was in with a genuine winning shot over such diverse distances. However, after qualifying third fastest, his self-belief was shattered by quarter final defeat to Belgian rider Jean Brankart. As he walked to the changing rooms, he broke down and wept on the shoulders of British team manager, Tommy

Godwin. Godwin comforted him and tried to bolster his belief for the 279-kilometre road race – 55 kilometres longer than any event he'd done before. In chaotic Simpson style, he had a minor fall between the two events, while riding his road bike with his track machine parallel, leaving him with a bandaged left arm for the big day.

His first professional World Championship road race took place among the sand dunes at Zandvoort on a sweltering August day. Simpson made it into an early, decisive eight-rider breakaway, which included Noel Foré, Michele Gismondi and French favourites Henry Anglade and André Darrigade. In front, he went through a see-saw psychological experience probably familiar to many other racing cyclists, from sitting in and thinking of excuses for when he quit to dealing with aching muscles and a headache. But going through more and more raging baptisms of fire,

Simpson lost the race, but won the hearts of the French public with a brave late move, 1960 Paris-Roubaix

Simpson proved able to stand the heat. He found second and third winds, even attacking in a failed last lap bid for victory.

Darrigade won the sprint easily, but Simpson's fourth place was the best Great Britain had ever done in the event's 32-year history. Yet, Simpson had a dissatisfaction befitting an established star. "Fourth has no official recognition. It was an empty feeling which descended upon me and I was once again depressed for I had truly been confident that I would finish 1959 as a world champion", he reflected later in *Cycling* magazine. It didn't help that the judges originally placed him sixth, after confusing his race number, 69, for that of number 89, the Dutchman Ab Geldermans.

As Muhammad Ali said, to be a great champion, you must first believe you are the best. If you're not, pretend you are. Simpson regularly possessed self-belief that bordered on arrogance:

he later claimed to "never be surprised when I win, only when I lose". Despite intermittent dazzling displays, the lessons and defeats came thick and fast during Simpson's salad days. Perhaps the harshest was at the Tour de l'Ouest at the end of July 1959, around Brittany. He had caught the eye of team manager Raymond Louviot and was guesting for his Rapha-Géminiani squad. It was the Briton's first outing against the sport's stars, including Rik Van Steenbergen, Jean Stablinski and Jean Forestier.

Simpson's attacking spirit was rewarded on day four to Quimper, when he bridged across to a breakaway and won, taking the race lead. In the next day's undulating 45-kilometre Breton time-trial, he claimed another victory. It should have been the coup de grâce: Simpson was two minutes clear of his closest challenger, well on course for a shock victory. There was a cruel twist.

Tucking into a sandwich, five minutes before the start of a Tour de l'Ouest stage, 1959. Photograph by Yvan Clench

1960 TOUR DE FRANCE: With
green jersey Jean Graczyk

1962 WORLD CHAMPIONSHIPS:
Simpson pulled out once he'd
missed the decisive breakaway in Salò, Italy

On the sixth stage, coincidentally finishing in his adopted home city of Saint-Brieuc, a small escape group containing his team-mate Job Morvan went up the road, plausibly as a watchman who would contribute next-to-no effort. The chase behind was half-hearted and Simpson was inconvenienced by an ill-timed puncture, having to switch to a team-mate's bicycle. When he got to the finish, Morvan had taken the race lead by five minutes. It was borderline betrayal, likely authorised by his team manager preferring an established Breton professional to take the spoils on home soil rather than an unknown foreigner. It took a considerable degree of complicity from other team-mates and riders too. As the French say, *il faut être pris pour être appris:* you need to be taken in to take it on board. It was an important insight into the cut-throat nature of the sport. Later, as a seasoned pro on Peugeot, it would be Simpson doing the taking.

Nevertheless, Simpson was seen as the moral victor and was courted by several top teams. Turning down offers from Margnat and Mercier, Simpson agreed a deal with the Saint-Raphaël-Géminiani team that summer, which would become Rapha-Gitane-Dunlop the following season. It was home to one of his childhood heroes, Brian Robinson, who would serve as his mentor for the next two years. When the 1959 Tour de France stopped in Rennes one afternoon, Simpson visited to sign his contract. Called down from his hotel room to translate the terms, Robinson was surprised to discover that this greenhorn was getting paid 800 francs a month – considerably more than him, a fourth-year professional and Tour de France stage winner. It turned out to be a canny bit of business.

Brian Robinson's piercing blue eyes flick through folders of cuttings and photographs on his dinner table in the Yorkshire town of Mirfield. They help him cast his mind back to the arrival of "the mad Englishman" on the scene. The first Briton to finish the Tour, alongside Tony Hoar in 1955, Robinson spent six years living and racing in Europe. He is the one who set the wheel turning for his countrymen, winning Tour de France stages in 1958 and 1959 and the 1961 Dauphiné Libéré. The godfather of British cycling has only received due recognition for his achievements in the last decade, aided by the sport's explosion of popularity and Olympic and Tour de France success. The French writer Antoine Blondin likened him to the Robinson Crusoe character Man Friday, "the savage who learns the gestures of our civilisation and who will in turn teach civilised cycling to his fellow savages."

Asked how he considers Simpson's place in the sport, Robinson pauses and replies "apprentice pioneer", with a laugh. He and Simpson were different characters, Robinson more reserved and phlegmatic, but they became friends and shared an apartment in Paris for 18 months. Robinson recalls that Simpson had no trouble ingratiating himself with new team-mates at the first Rapha-Gitane-Dunlop training camp at Palavas-Plage in January 1960. "He was always jovial. He made fun of anybody, himself included", Robinson says. "His character was very lively. You couldn't fall out with Tom."

He proffers a photograph from the training camp's leaving party, which illustrates this. Sat around a dinner table, Simpson on the right is laughing uproariously as Nicolas Barone holds court. Fellow team-mates Robinson, Michel Dejouhannet, Pierre Everaert and the "three lovely daughters" who lived there are all smiling too.

Befitting its aperitif sponsor, the Rapha team was a curious cocktail of French talent, the British odd couple, the Dutch duo of Ab Geldermans and Jo de Haan, plus the German Altig brothers.

"We never had a top dog, to be honest", Robinson says. "Guys like Roger Rivière, Raphaël Géminiani and myself were respected a bit more than everyone else. So they were all sort of protected in the early days of a stage race. But if they didn't have the form, they didn't get looked after because we were a young team and we were always the best prize winners because we were all hungry. We all needed to make money

60

Simpson races the individual pursuit at the World Track Championships in Zurich, 1961. In future years, he would occasionally wear a warming plaster on his knee to help ward off a recurring injury sustained that summer

so there was an automatic shared workload."

Robinson says he had no envy of Simpson, a second Briton on the scene. "As far as I was concerned, he was a breath of fresh air because I was in a rut. I was already 30, I was at my peak when Tom came along and there's always a role [for you to play]. I looked after him quite a bit." He admits that on their first camp in January 1960, he'd be quite glad to ride alongside a different partner, such was the barrage of questions he'd be getting from the inquisitive newcomer.

While avuncular and light-hearted, Robinson retains a steel about him. He stopped at nothing to make a success of his sporting career: as a young professional, he sold his car to make some money for one last shot at Europe. Cycling was a precarious living for all but the sport's stars. Salaries were paid by bigger teams, but they only provided makeweight earnings. The real money came from contracts for criterium races or prize money. However, that could be tardy. "It went to the federation in France and then the federation

in England; it would be winter time when I got it", Robinson says. "You wouldn't count on that. You counted on the primes you won each year and were given after the race. The rest, I just sort of survived with … I had to guarantee 20 criteriums after the Tour, which were well paid."

The contracts for these were arranged by agents, who took a cut of the fee – usually 10 per cent – for themselves. Robinson and Simpson were in the stable of Daniel Dousset, the most influential agent of the time, alongside the likes of leading riders Jacques Anquetil, Louison Bobet and Roger Rivière. He was rarely far from a charge's side after wins, ready to capitalise right away: after Simpson's failed breakaway at the 1960 Paris-Roubaix, a photograph shows the glassy-eyed protagonist staring right at the lens, while the debonair Dousset stands next to him in an overcoat and cravatte. As the ones with the keys to the cash register, these smooth operators held considerable sway in the sport. At one Paris-Nice, the Italian star Vittorio Adorni raced for his fellow Dousset stablemate Anquetil, putting aside personal and team ambitions.

Often at criteriums, the best riders – the *grands coureurs* – had a monopoly. They would decide between themselves who would win and impose their will on lesser riders. According to Simpson's fellow rider Vin Denson, it was the case in competitive races on occasions. "When Tom was young, he used to get people really vicious, having a go at him, because he used to attack too often", he says. "Often, other riders would get together, like Altig and Anquetil, to put him in his place until he was accepted: make sure that nobody worked with him and he didn't do anything. They didn't like riders who went against what they wanted to do." How did he gain their acceptance? "When he won all those Classics."

Simpson adapted quickly during his meteoric rise, a necessity in a sport where a rider's value fluctuates constantly, like stock prices, based on potential and short-term performances. Back then, slow developers would be at a loss in a milieu that demanded quick results and ruthless self-interest. "Cycling is a bit of a rat race", Simpson says in *The World of Tommy Simpson* film. "But then if you're with the top rats' teams earning, say, £10,000 a year, you can bear it."

For Simpson, it was a simple equation: attacks or results meant publicity for his sponsor and for himself, publicity meant contracts and contracts meant money. While his 1960 Paris-Roubaix breakaway brought him a slew of race invitations and mainstream attention, it was the biggest in a sequence of spring escapes which had included Genoa-Roma and Milan-Sanremo. Several times that season, he was touted as the new Ferdi Kübler by the French media for his flamboyant racing and resemblance to the Swiss Tour de France champion. Simpson's emergence in 1960 was a rare sunny moment for the Rapha-Gitane-Dunlop team in a dark season. Team captain Roger Rivière, who held the Hour Record and had won two stages at the previous year's Tour de France, broke his back in a crash at the Tour and was forced to retire at the age of 24; the painkiller palfium was later found in his back pocket. Meanwhile, his team-mate and fellow prodigy Gérard Saint died in a car crash that spring.

When Simpson's performances weren't enough to earn column inches, he had his nationality to fall back on. Initially, he was happy to ham up the urbane, bowler-wearing English stereotype, which earned him the tag of Mister Tom. Flourishes of his *humour anglais* were lapped up by the press pack. According to a watching *L'Equipe* writer at the 1960 Genoa-Roma, as Simpson took a newspaper at the summit of one climb to stuff down his jersey for warmth, he said: "I'll never have time to read this on the descent."

He also did a fine line in posing ostentatiously for press photographs, whether it was riding a donkey in Dunkirk or donning a sombrero in France. That way, he could be both the clown of the circus and its results-seizing ringleader. "He might have pushed it a little bit as you probably would, but it was natural. He was born that way", Robinson says.

On the bike, rookie mistakes still needed erasing. Simpson had a habit of switching onto smaller sprockets, making pedalling harder, to power away from the bunch on climbs with a slower cadence. It was brutally effective in the short run, but murder on the legs and no way to get through a Tour de France.

On his debut in 1960, the young talent was like a Catherine wheel, flying up the road several times before the mountains, shining brightly then flickering and dying as the race wore on. A steady burner, Robinson regularly advised him to measure his efforts in long stage races, in order to finish as strongly as he started. The Yorkshireman gave him counsel on everything from the organisation of his suitcase to getting as much sleep as possible: as the saying goes, the Tour is won in bed. Whether the gung-ho apprentice heeded his master's advice was another matter. "He wouldn't take any bloody notice; he'd do what he wanted", Robinson says. "You go through life and you think 'I've done that daft, I won't do it again.' That's how Tom learned really: by mistakes."

Often driven by impulse, Simpson was a loose cannon. "I wouldn't say I was a particularly intelligent rider because I get carried away too often. I can't bear to sit and wait for a chance. I like to make it", he reflects in *The World of Tommy*

Getting carried away on another long breakaway, 1960 Milan-Sanremo

Simpson. This propensity for the spectacular often made his victories especially memorable. However, such combativity complicated his ambitions to win the Tour de France. It was a race that demanded pragmatism and careful energy conservation from contenders. The frosty, functional Jacques Anquetil had that down to a tee, winning the race five times between 1957 and 1964.

However, as the entertainer in a gaggle of watchmen, Simpson's contrasting traits endeared him to the public during this period. If not quite untying Anquetil's cravatte tourniquet around the Tour, he loosened it and humanised the racing. Simpson was an inveterate battler, the taker of unnecessary risks, *le forcené de l'attaque* – the breakaway maniac.

His directeur sportif, Raymond Louviot, regularly tried to temper Simpson's attacking tendencies. A French champion and Tour de France stage winner in the 1930s, Louviot was a canny tactician who commanded respect. Akin to a professor dealing with an *enfant terrible*, he could be left alternately delighted by Simpson's panache one day and exasperated by his scatterbrain moves the next.

Robinson describes Louviot as "fair, but Jekyll and Hyde". The diminutive manager wasn't afraid to give Simpson a piece of his mind when he felt he had erred. He was present at the Sachsenring in 1960 for the World Championship road race, where the Briton was an outside bet for victory. While World Championships were raced in national teams, the chief beneficiaries in publicity from a high finish would have been Rapha-Gitane-Dunlop.

In the race's early stages, Simpson's shoelace broke. He eased to the back of the group and stopped to tie it up, at which point a braking following car knocked him over, causing him to hit his head on the tarmac. Race over, he headed to the medical tent for stitches. Spectating after competing in the amateur race, his old Olympic team-mate Billy Holmes followed him there and remembers what happened next: "Louviot was trying to hit Simpson, he was bollocking him. Doctors were holding him back. I can't speak French but my first wife could. Louviot was going:

'Simpson! You do not pay attention to detail. Tonight, you would have been world champion. Next year, you would have been a rich, rich man. And what are you? Nothing but a fool. A foolish Englishman.' And Simpy's having stitches put in while all this is happening."

The incident epitomised Simpson's crash course first season; he later reckoned that he had fallen as many as 16 times in races during 1960. Few racers arrive in the pro world to the manner born; even Eddy Merckx was ropey downhill as a new professional. Simpson was no different. "He had to learn to ride his bike", Brian Robinson says. "He wasn't a good descender, his movements were too sharp and they weren't controlled enough; his reflexes might have been too quick." The nail-biting nature of his first stage race win as a professional, at the 1960 Tour du Sud-Est, owed a great deal to inexperience. After getting into a breakaway on the opening stage and staying in contention over Mont Ventoux, Simpson was third going into the final day from Marseille to Bandol, taking in Mont Faron. Six weeks earlier, he had won a time-trial up the famous Mediterranean climb, putting minutes into the great Charly Gaul; on this day, he was lagging behind as the race exploded. Up front, his rival René Privat was away in a breakaway, with the race win in his hands.

Brian Robinson dropped back to help his young compatriot. "We were going down a hill I knew quite well and Tom fell off", he recalls. "I slowed down, he got back on and I said: 'sit on my wheel Tom, I know where I'm going.' He bloody fell off again, didn't he?"

Despite his cuts and scrapes, Simpson attacked on the Grand-Caunet hill, 40 kilometres from the finish, with the help of Roger Rivière. His directeur sportif Louviot drove to the front and demanded that another team-mate in the breakaway, Raymond Mastrotto, drop back to aid the Briton's pursuit too. Noting this, the Mercier directeur sportif Antonin Magne told his charge Privat to give it everything he had in front.

With five kilometres to go, the deficit had reduced sufficiently in Simpson's favour: Privat stayed away to win the battle, but not the war.

63

1960 TOUR DE
FRANCE:
Being interviewed by a
reporter before a stage

1960 TOUR DE
FRANCE:

A pipe and a smile ahead
of stage 9

Climbing the Col de
Luitel, 1960 Tour
de France, stage 17
between Briançon and
Aix-les-Bains

There was still time for one more scare as Simpson crashed again on the cobbles of Marseille's Old Port, a couple of kilometres from the finish.

Only the tears were missing, as the sweaty, bloodied Simpson chased back on for his narrow victory. His courageous comeback ensured more coverage in the French newspapers, yet his soaring profile didn't sit well with his peers. "Before victory came my way at the Tour du Sud-Est, I was to be the most unpopular rider in our usually close-knit team. Oddly enough, my unpopularity really stemmed from the fact that I was becoming increasingly popular with the public", he later wrote in *Cycling*. "Great publicity being given to Mister Tom was reflecting itself back to my rivals, with the result that I was becoming more and more of a marked man."

Louviot entered Simpson in the subsequent Midi Libre, a Tour de France warm-up race in south-west France. Swathed in bandages and exhausted, the last thing he wanted or needed was another race. So, he abandoned on the first day, hiding from his directeur sportif like a truant schoolboy. "Has Louviot gone past yet? Yes?" Simpson asked *L'Equipe* journalist Robert Silva. "I'll stay here, he won't come back to look for me. I can't carry on, I'm afraid of crashing, I've got enough injuries and dead fingers from the effort of braking."

The relentless racing schedule was another element for Simpson's body to get used to. From the hundreds of kilometres clocked on January training camps to non-stop travel and strenuous week-long races piled on top of another, his body was taking on an unprecedented workload. With that in mind, Louviot had advised him not to start his first Tour de France in 1960, which was contested by national teams then. However, reminded of the money he could make for himself

Another impetuous crash at the finish of stage five in St. Malo, 1960 Tour de France

there by his manager Dousset, Simpson felt that it was a race he couldn't refuse. "Tom was always keen on money. You have to be. He came with bugger all to start with, like most of us did", Brian Robinson says. At the start of the Tour, he was already feeling burned out by the relentless season; by its finish in Paris, he was deadbeat.

Robinson and Simpson went separate ways at the end of 1961: Simpson moved to Ghent in Belgium, Robinson left cycling and returned to Mirfield and the building trade. "The only thing that worried me about Tom was how much he indulged in the drugs scene. He didn't talk to me about it, but there we are", Robinson says. Did he go out and actively look for them? "I think so. Well, he went to Belgium and that's where it all came from at the time. It was all pills in France then; the syringes came out in Belgium." Some of this appears to be circumstantial speculation,

as Robinson says that Simpson "certainly was not on drugs when I knew him." How would he have known that, for sure? "From the contents of his jersey when he came home."

The protégé went on to surpass the pioneer. If Robinson was the British cyclist who first hacked a route through this tangled, overgrown jungle, occasionally able to twist its law to his own benefit, then Simpson was its first conqueror. Did his later achievements surprise Robinson? "Surprised isn't the right word. Impressed, certainly. You expect everybody to rise until they come up against something. Tom was in the right place, which you've got to be. But so were a lot of other people, and they didn't make it like he did. He had the class, that's all. I was a good bike rider but I was never a champion as such. These guys are that bit more special. It would be wrong to say it could come out of a bottle. You've got to have that class, even if you've taken drugs."

67

68 69

Chapter Four

HELEN AND TOM

Helen Hoban sits in darkness by her living room window. She looks out over green, sheep-strewn Welsh pastures, bathed in the blue sky of an unseasonably warm October day. "So, you're writing a book, is it?" she says, turning to greet me. Moving out of the shadow, her features become clearer. She is tall and fine, her arms bronzed by a recent holiday. The Dusty Springfield-esque beehive hairdo she had in the Sixties is now dyed blonde and around her shoulders; the butterfly glasses have been replaced for a more modern pair. She is not quite as fast as the days when she used to win the mothers' race at sports day either, limping around with a medical boot, due to a drawn-out recovery from a broken leg.

To most, Tom Simpson is an abstract figure, a cycling champion admired or admonished from afar. Few have a better appreciation of his character than the Hobans: Helen was his wife, his confidante, the mother of their children; arguably, the person who knew him the best. Two years after Simpson's death, she married his friend and team-mate Barry Hoban, who became one of the most prolific British racing cyclists in history.

During two interviews at the Hobans' stone-walled farmhouse above the Welsh town of Newtown, certain memories provoke a waterfall of words, as if flinging open a portal and taking them vividly back to those moments, five decades ago. Helen Sherburn, as she was back then, clearly remembers meeting Tom in April 1959, and for more than just his boyish good looks. "I knew there was something in him, a drive. That he really wanted to have a go at it", she says. "From the way he talked. He was really positive and very focused on his racing. He knew what he wanted and how he would get it."

It wasn't love at first sight. "I didn't want to come in between him and the racing at all. No, no, no. I could see where he was going, but I was behind him all the way, standing back a bit. I could see he didn't want to have anything that would take his mind off cycling. Like a girlfriend."

An English gent in Ghent, 1965

I ask what the pair had in common. She pauses and searches her mind. "We didn't have very much, actually", Helen says. "You must have had something", Barry interjects. "You're a bit of a perfectionist at heart, Tom was a perfectionist in his sport. Things have got to be right for you." They shared a taste for adventure too. A teenage girl from Doncaster did not lightly head off to mainland Europe for months in the late Fifties. But while working in the local Boots store, Helen was dreaming of learning the languages, so off she went.

Though far more *au fait* with French than Simpson after spending several months there, the world of cycling was alien to Helen. She never saw him race during his spell in Brittany; on one day off work, she walked for several kilometres to the neighbouring town of Yffiniac to see an event, only to realise that Simpson wasn't there.

For her, there was a sense of wonder in sending letters to far-flung race headquarters and having them magically reach Simpson, wherever he was. Helen still has their correspondence in the loft and reads it occasionally. One letter from the 1959 Tour de l'Ouest shows how formal their early relationship was. "He put at the end 'yours sincerely, Tom Simpson.' Ha!" she says, with a little high-pitched laugh. "So you can imagine: he was focused on the cycling. But I think he must have liked me."

She was right. After Helen left to work in the German town of Kornwestheim, absence made Simpson's heart grow fonder. They exchanged letters and in the winter of 1959, Simpson realised that he had fallen for her while talking with his friends one day. He retells the endearing moment in his autobiography: "'I met a lovely girl in France. She was English too,' and as soon as I had said it, I knew I was in love with her and there was nobody else for me."

Given the distance, letter-writing was their main form of communication. On a rare occasion when Helen went to see Simpson finish the 1960 Tour de France at the Parc des Princes, he tested the Marilyn Monroe quote "if you can't handle me at my worst, then you sure as hell don't deserve me

71

at my best". Simpson was exhausted, emaciated and sporting facial scars from a bizarre tumble with team-mate Brian Robinson. One morning before a stage, Simpson was leaning on his bike, chatting to a journalist, when Robinson crashed into him, sending him flying.

After the season ended, Simpson could fully focus on romance. He turned up unannounced on Helen's doorstep in late November 1960, having driven hundreds of kilometres to see her. "I was absolutely gobsmacked when he arrived. I had no idea he was coming", she says. The Diller family, for whom she was working, gave them use of their weekend house in the Black Forest for several days. "I made this egg and radish salad one day, I think I used 12 eggs for the two of us!" she says, laughing.

Within six weeks of their German holiday, they were married. "It sort of just happened", Helen says. "He didn't get down on one knee, nothing like that. He went to Doncaster to buy the ring and we said we would get married the following October. Then Tom said 'no, I'm not waiting that long. We'll do it before I go down to the training camp in the south of France.' So we had to rush a bit to go to the priest and ask him for a special licence, because we got married on the third of January 1961. This is just how Tom was: very spontaneous." And it was always Tom to her, despite the media's preference for the longer alias. "He didn't like Tommy, I don't like Tommy either", she says.

The Christmas cake was ingeniously repurposed, its original decorations scraped off and replaced by a model bride and groom for the small ceremony. The next day, they travelled to London for the Daily Mirror Sportsman's Dinner, where Simpson showed the ring to Brian Robinson. Such was the speed of their matrimony, he thought it was another stitch-up from the perennial joker. There wasn't time for a honeymoon: after a few days staying at the shared apartment in Paris, Helen went back to work in Germany and Simpson was off training and racing in the south of France. They didn't see one another for two months.

Camping out by Lake Zurich with Helen for the 1961 World Championships

With prime minister
Harold Wilson at the
reception for BBC
Sports Personality of
the Year, 1965

Subsequently, Helen permanently moved into their cramped bolthole on 222 Rue Martissot, in the north-west Parisian suburb of Clichy, just beyond the *périphérique* ring road. "Eleventh floor. No lift", she recalls. "There was no dining room or living room, just two bedrooms. We had one and Brian and [his first wife] Shirley had the other. Tom was just starting to earn some money and we didn't have all the mod cons in those days. It was a tiny little kitchen, with no washing machine, so I had this big pan that I used to put on top of the gas cooker. I'd boil all the clothes in there, then I'd

have to wring them out. When Tom came home, I used to like to make things nice from what we had. I used to cook meals and put serviettes and candles out on the little table there."

During the season, Simpson was rarely back for long, due to the staccato rhythm of races and travel. Helen would get the Metro into Paris and walk down the Champs-Elysées and the Rue Saint-Honoré, looking around the shops. "I could never afford anything, but it was just lovely", she says. "I did it all on my own, quite often." She particularly remembers the friendliness of the old

74

A little training session in the garage with daughters Jane and Joanne, 1966

couple in the flat below, who would sometimes invite her downstairs for lamb roasts with flageolet beans. With a negligible social calendar and absent husband, it was a lonely, abnormal life for a young woman. But then, behind every champion cyclist is a self-sacrificing partner. "I didn't think of it is as detrimental. That was the life we knew", Helen says. "I recognised that you had to forfeit nice things like going away on holiday, because I knew that in the end, it would be beneficial for us all."

When asked if she ever worried about where money would come from, there is faint surprise in her voice as she replies: "It didn't enter my head really that he hadn't got much money. I never doubted him at all."

The son of a mine worker, Simpson was one of many in the peloton who came from humble stock, looking to make a healthy living. While a 250-kilometre race in sweltering heat or freezing rain was no bed of roses, it was still an easier way of making ends meet than other hardships of the era. The Spanish climber extraordinaire, Federico Bahamontes, had a job breaking rocks at the side of the road and occasionally ate cats

75

as an adolescent in Franco-era Spain; meanwhile, Simpson's rival Gianni Motta came from abject poverty in a north Italian village. His family slept in one room and lived on polenta. When Simpson visited his house, he noticed chicken wire around the table and fowl clucking about on the dirt floor, picking up fallen crumbs.

Unsurprisingly, top cyclists could be ruthless and parsimonious: when you've come from nothing and glimpsed El Dorado, you especially don't want to go back to nothing. Even Jacques Anquetil, with his bourgeois airs and taste for the good life, was the son of a Norman strawberry farmer who toiled in the fields picking fruit. He was a prime example of self-transformation and social mobility through sport for Simpson. Mixing style on the bicycle with substantial success, the Frenchman won five Tours de France, commanded a lucrative criterium fee and met the likes of Yuri Gagarin, Charles De Gaulle and Sugar Ray Robinson. His wife Janine was a paragon for Helen too. "Every month, I read *Miroir du Cyclisme* and I used to admire Madame Anquetil and Jean Stablinski's wife, their elegance. I used to think 'oh my God!' They were completely different to me. I suppose they were the WAGs of that time." Within a few years, the Simpsons would be in their circle.

Wives were not expected to be at the epicentre of cycling races. This was an era where, as Ian Fleming's spy James Bond says in *Casino Royale*, women were expected to "mind their pots and pans, stick to their frocks and gossip and leave men's work to the men." In this patriarchal sport, traditional attitudes reigned: sharing rooms at professional races was out of the question and sex in the lead-up to big races was discouraged, as if it might steal vital reserves (modern science has since proven this to be nonsense). The fairer sex was more likely to be represented in the form of eye candy: podium girls beaming in sponsors' sashes, scantily clad dancers at track meets or the groupies who followed the races. There was a practical reason for Helen's absence too: for most of Simpson's career, they couldn't afford for her to accompany him. She held the fort, paying the bills and raising their two daughters.

However, she was far more than a sporting Stepford wife, often pulled directly into this sporting world. With her superior written French, she helped to arrange a meeting and potential contract for Simpson's friend Vin Denson in the winter of 1963 with Peugeot manager Gaston Plaud, though a rule on the number of foreigners ultimately scuppered the transfer. She filled in to collect awards for Simpson in the autumn of 1965, when he was committed to racing elsewhere. She sewed bits of cloth onto his track shorts, which his racing partner would often use to hurl himself into the race with more momentum, and washed his kit. Just as well: at one race soon after his World Championship victory, Simpson did it himself and ended up shrinking the woollen rainbow jersey to comical proportions.

One of her old German leather handbags even ended up being reappropriated by Simpson as an ingenious way of improving the comfort of his Unica saddle. She didn't mind. "It was an old one", Helen says.

Following from a distance, she commiserated the many defeats; Helen was so sympathetic over the phone to Simpson after a 1963 Liège-Bastogne-Liège loss, where he was caught in the final kilometres, that he burst into tears down the receiver. At other times, Simpson could be tense and short with her. "When he'd not done very well and come home, I knew not to talk to him. Leave him be on his own", she says. "What aggravated him was some little thing. And he would just go off the deep end. But it didn't last very long."

Simpson was racing in the gutter, looking up at the stars for several years and their battle for financial security was hard-fought. The 1961 season emphasised the central role of the Tour de France in this. Though Simpson won the prestigious Tour of Flanders in March, a nagging knee injury led to an early abandon in the sport's biggest race and he was not invited to many subsequent criteriums. Out of contract with Saint-Raphaël that autumn and nearly broke, Simpson was signed by Gitane-Leroux. The transfer coincided with the family's move to Ghent and a loaned cottage from businessman friend René Halliez on the Pantserschipstraat. Attached to a coal merchant's yard, it sat by the Terneuzen sea canal, in view of the ships coming and going from one of Belgium's busiest ports and the nearby industrial chimneys, belching out smoke. The house was a few kilometres from the city centre, but a very long way from its Gothic charm.

"There was a really fishy smell from the chemical factory down the road. Every time you hung your washing out, it smelled. Ugh, it was horrible. Well, it wasn't horrible, it was a

house for us", Helen says. "When we first lived there, we had nothing. We earned everything we bought. I remember Tom said to me 'right, we need a three-piece suite so we'll go and get one.' I sat on that sofa and it was just a dream, an absolute dream", she says, moving her hands by her sides as if feeling the invisible fabric. "Everything we got was a dream." It was a hand-to-mouth existence. In late 1962, the family moved to a bigger house in Ghent's Mariakerke district and Simpson joined Peugeot. Even then, the French team hedged its bets on him; he only

Still smiling on the way to a Majorca training camp, despite breaking his leg skiing, 1966

signed an official contract after racing with them for an entire season.

Despite the constant anxiety over money, Simpson had a habit of making frivolous purchases. During his first years in France, he splashed out on an Aston Martin DB4 and a DB2. They looked the part, but the gas guzzlers were ill-suited to the long drives he regularly had to make. While Simpson was impulsive, he also possessed supreme self-belief. He was right to reckon that their status would soon catch up with these prematurely bought symbols. He would use them as carrots on sticks to chase; before leaving for the fateful 1967 Tour de France, he'd put a down-payment on another Mercedes. "He was a nutter on cars. We had BMWs and Jags too", Helen says, laughing. "Let's put it this way, he wouldn't consult me before he went to buy a car."

"It did worry me", Helen says, of his propensity to buy things without checking. Would she tell him it wasn't a good move and request that he check with her next time? "No, because I knew he would be happy. I never used to say that."

For a man who seemingly lived life at full speed, it's perhaps no surprise that Simpson's driving left much to be desired; his friend and fellow racing cyclist Neville Veale says the Briton harboured ambitions of becoming a rally driver. Many cyclists, accustomed to white-knuckle descents and the ragged edge of the bicycle race, are devils behind a steering wheel.

"It frightened the life out of me", Helen says. "I remember one time, no word of a lie, I was all for opening the door and jumping out. This was coming from Geneva to Saint-Gervais, we'd been to pick somebody up from the airport and he was going round these bends like absolute crazy. We were almost on two wheels. I was so afraid. 'Well, we've got to get there'", she says, imitating Tom.

Her cries to slow down didn't register. "Not in the slightest. If there was going to be a divorce, then that was the day," she adds wryly. However, she believes that Tom was at his happiest on their winter skiing trips in the mid-Sixties. They were brief moments of relaxation, away from the

Helen and Tom take skis out of their Mercedes, 1964

demands of the racing season, where they joined the families of fellow champions Jan Janssen and Jacques Anquetil on the piste at Saint-Gervais. "Before he broke his leg", Helen adds. There's often a caveat with Simpson. "He says 'I'll meet you at Le Bettex,' which was halfway down the slope", she recalls of the January 1966 incident. "I wasn't a good skier at all, Tom wasn't… well, he'd do anything. I was just coming out of the ski lift to go down and somebody said 'quick, quick, the ambulance.' I thought, 'some stupid idiot's gone and fallen.' And it was Tom."

He broke his leg and ended up in a hospital in Sallanches, a stone's throw away from where he finished fourth in the World Championships 16 months previously. It was a disaster for the reigning rainbow jersey at the height of his sporting and earning powers: a couple of months recovering meant he had to forfeit several lucrative racing contracts and sacrificed his chances of a high finish at the spring Classics.

Helen reckons that it wasn't until his 1964 triumph at Milan-Sanremo that the pair were financially comfortable. She recalls crying down the phone to him afterwards: not just with joy at the result, but for the long-term consequences. Simpson sought to secure their future wealth with property purchases: 22 acres of land in Corsica, a house near Doncaster and the construction of two apartments on the outskirts of Ghent. Since his teenage days when he would sell on mail-order cycling products from the Hertfordshire-based JD Whisker to his peers, he had an eye for a deal. Later, he would take European jerseys and tracksuits back to Britain for sale, which were treasured by aspiring racing cyclists there.

In 1965, his victories at the World Championships and Tour of Lombardy took the Simpsons to the greatest heights of fame and fortune. Helen had gone from working as an au pair to employing their own to look after the children. They enjoyed après-ski with singer Petula Clark, and met the Queen when she came to Brussels: they had gone from rank-and-file to royalty. Being a self-made couple was special. "We came from nothing. I was very proud of that and always will be. Tom was very proud too", Helen says.

At times, even as she recalls it now, Helen seems to wonder whether this all really happened. It was surreal back then too. In a *Sunday Times* feature, the journalist Desmond Zvar captures a conversation between her and Tom in November 1965, the day after being driven down crowd-packed streets to Ghent town hall in a horse-drawn landau for Tom to receive the freedom of the city:

Helen: "I could never have believed all this would happen."

Tom: "Why? Didn't you have any faith in me?"

Helen: "Well, love, when we married we had nothing, you know… it's all sort of so hard to believe."

But then, Simpson was a man of vivid reveries who liked to tame the seemingly impossible. He fancied building a house in Normandy, and later dreamed of getting one on Lake Garda if a discussed move to an Italian team came off. After their property purchases, the ideas became more abstract: he dreamed of owning a house with a tree going through it, of living on a plane, a train and even owning a 50-foot catamaran. "My wife thinks I'm crazy, but I'd like to have a charter yacht with me as captain", he told *Cycling* in 1967. "I'd live in Corsica and do trips with the tourists." Simpson never got to retirement, but it certainly wouldn't have been dull.

His sudden death on Mont Ventoux during the 1967 Tour de France turned Helen's world upside down. Time can lighten such a huge emotional load, but it is a weight that perhaps never fully lifts. "Why? Why? If I had been there, I wouldn't have put him back on the bike," she says. As she speaks, her fists are tightened and she stares at the window, between Barry opposite her and me to the right. Several of her sentences trail off without endings. "I would never have put him back on the bike. And I ask myself all these questions. Surely he could have seen what was happening but… just to leave myself, Jane and Joanne… I was really angry with Tom. But I'm not angry now."

Joanne and Jane were four and five years old respectively when their father died, but despite their fleeting memories of him, the similarities are uncanny. "Joanne has just got exactly his temperament, exactly his guts, exactly his determination. It's hard to believe. Jane, the eldest daughter, looked like him in every way when she was born. She had lots of black hair; the hairline was the same." Suddenly, Helen is louder, almost shouting: "So as far as I'm concerned, he will never *ever* die. Because every time I look at my kids, Tom comes through in them."

Given the 50 years that have passed, Helen marvels at Simpson's revered modern status and embraces the constant reminders of him that pop up. She revels in browsing Tom Simpson groups on Facebook, treasuring fresh anecdotes and unseen photographs. However, his posthumous portrayal is a double-edged sword. The broad painting of Simpson as a drugs cheat has contributed to her apprehension of journalists. At times, Helen's tension is clear from her deep breaths and body language, as if she expects me to broadside her with a sudden, scandalous question. "It is hurtful. I find that I just can't talk about it", she says, when I mention doping.

Letting everything fade quietly into the past would be easier and more painless, but the Hobans like to celebrate the happy times shared. "With Tom, we don't talk in whispers. Tom is in the memory of our household", Barry says. Over the years, Mont Ventoux has become a place of pilgrimage rather than pain. "I wish that we lived nearer and I could visit it more often. That's my one regret", Helen says, adding later: "I want my ashes thrown on there."

Simpson is gone, but he still lives on in her consciousness. "I have a reccurring dream," Helen says. "Tom walks in. And I say to him 'where have you been? Where *have* you been all this time?' In the very beginning, not so much now, Tom came into my dream and we were living a normal life, but I was trying to hide Barry in the wardrobe. I'll wake up one morning and say to Barry, 'I've had another dream about Tom, the same one. Tom was back.'"

Helen with her father Frank (left) and Tom's sister Peggy (right) at his funeral, 1967

Chapter Five

MONUMENT MAN

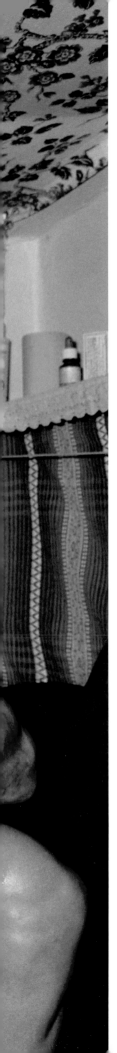

The glamour of the
Six Day racing scene

A fortnight after Tom Simpson rocketed to Tour of Flanders victory in 1961, Yuri Gagarin became the first man in Space. It's difficult to say which achievement was more inconceivable. The Vostok mission was a ground-breaking feat for mankind, but a logical next step in the escalating Space Race. Whereas far closer to home, Simpson's success was even more out of this world to the cycling fraternity.

"It was quite something because Englishmen were never expected to win, they were expected to lose", Simpson said, several years later. Over the next six years, he banished British cycling's inferiority complex and established himself and the country as a force in the sport with his brilliance in its most prestigious one-day races, the Monuments.

They consist of Milan-Sanremo, the Tour of Flanders, Paris-Roubaix, Liège-Bastogne-Liège and the Tour of Lombardy. All numbering between 250 and 290 kilometres in distance, each has its own history and demands different degrees of endurance, timing, fortune, teamwork and bike-handling ability. Simpson made them his forte. The Briton's wispy build concealed deceptive versatility: with his dazzling leg speed, desire and power, he was a threat on body-juddering cobbles or short, steep hills.

This all-rounder won three of the sport's holy quintet and came close to triumph in the other two, with lone breakaways snuffed out within kilometres of the finish at the 1960 Paris-Roubaix and 1963 Liège-Bastogne-Liège. Then, there was his 1965 success at Bordeaux-Paris, a race that defies categorisation, mixing marathon endurance and pacing behind derny motorbikes across a swathe of middle France.

As a whole, it is Simpson's Monument record which made him a champion of his time and still keeps him as Britain's greatest one-day racing cyclist.

1961 Tour of Flanders

The only similarity between the faded victory photograph and the present day is the tall, turreted water tower that looms in the background. Painted a shade of cyan blue that matches the autumn sky, it reassures me that I am in the right place. Otherwise, the trappings of modernity have sprung up and altered that finish line scene in Wetteren. There's a train track to the left side of the road, a green-liveried Power petrol station and parking bays occupied by a couple of coaches to the right.

A bike lane, part of the East Flanders network, makes up part of the beige pavement. A man at a perpendicular angle on a Segway – the wonders of two-wheeled innovation – whizzes past, alongside a few other town bike riders. Despite the passage of time, there's no mistaking it: this is the finishing location of the 1961 Tour of Flanders on the Warandelaan. It feels like there ought to be a monument to Britain's first modern Monument win here. As it is, next to nobody knows that one of the most controversial finishes in the Tour of Flanders history even took place here, on this quiet main road spiriting drivers out of town towards Dendermonde.

Known as *De Ronde van Vlaanderen* to locals, this race was a cipher for Flemish identity, a symbol of resilience and fierce pride. It was born in 1913 out of a groundswell of feeling for the native people and language. The idea of the Flandrian cycling champion became an enduring motif, of tough, hulking, silent men whose grim strength mirrored the atmosphere of great cities like Ghent and Bruges.

"Cycling here in Belgium *is* Flanders, and it's the race of the Flandrians. They prepare for the Tour of Flanders as if it is the World Championships", says Emile Daems, Simpson's former Peugeot team-mate who won Milan-Sanremo, the Tour of Lombardy and Paris-Roubaix in the early Sixties. "A big champion always wins the Tour of Flanders. You need to have a bit of luck, but you need to know how to ride, to be tough and you need to understand Flanders."

The peloton passes windmills and waterways, 1961 Tour of Flanders

The Tour of Flanders
skirts the sand
dunes of the North
Sea, 1961

The Tour of Flanders had a considerably less climb-packed route than the relentless modern course. But what it lacked in number of hills, it made up for in nerves, wind and distance. Setting off to Ostend and De Panne from the start city of Ghent, the gusts blowing off the North Sea could break the race up before it headed inland to Wetteren via six steep bergs, the last of which, in 1961, was the Grotenberge. With most riders eye-wateringly over-geared, a contender needed to stay near the front of the bunch due to the risk of crashing or being halted by a roadblock of riders walking up the cobbles.

"It is a race of two halves. You go out to the coast and round for the first 150 kilometres, then those bloody hills: they're nothing much, but they're cobbled, they're short, hard and if you get stopped… it's a pain in the arse", British cyclist Vin Denson, who raced several Tours of Flanders during the Sixties, says.

In 1961, Simpson arrived for the race from a narrow defeat at Menton-Roma, with words of wisdom fresh in his mind from the Swiss great Ferdi Kübler: "You are not a sprinter, but you are strong. Make the most of your punch. Accelerate once, twice, three times if you need to in the last kilometre to put the fast man in the wind and force him to make efforts. This way, you'll win races, and big ones too." Simpson did not possess a venomous finishing sprint, but he had the ability to put in repeated hard efforts at the end of a race.

However, Simpson started the 1961 Tour of Flanders with ropey legs. He crawled along for the first 100 kilometres, as did the rest of the bunch, racing into a headwind. After a crash, Simpson thought of abandoning, but his team-mate René Fournier geed him up. Pre-race favourite Rik Van Looy was not so fortunate, taken out in another incident.

Just after the halfway mark, Emile Daems, Camille Le Menn, Mies Stolker and Simpson's team-mate, Jo de Haan, escaped. Simpson's strength and willing showed: after a failed earlier attempt to escape the peloton, he broke clear with the Italian star Nino Defilippis on the Edelareberg with 55 kilometres to go. His directeur sportif Raymond Louviot told him to not work with the Italian as they bridged across to the breakaway, something he was at liberty to do, given that de Haan was in front. Simpson sometimes wasted his energy by riding excessively on the front, but on this day in April 1961, he would show the extent of his sangfroid and racing nous.

After the pair latched on, Daems thought Simpson would be giving his all to keep it together for the faster-finishing De Haan. There was no reaction when Simpson made his move with Defilippis, five kilometres from the finish. By the time Daems realised his mistake, they were 200 metres down the road and the following cars helped to stymie his chase. The next day, the Belgian dubbed it "the biggest error of my career". His fate shows the fickleness of the sport at that time. The Brussels resident had been a three-time Monument winner by the age of 25. However, a couple of fallow seasons and a broken hip left him without a team for 1967, three years later. He retired from the sport and ran a fish shop for the rest of his working life.

On the short finishing circuit around Wetteren, neither leader had reckoned on a quirk of fate: the fierce Flemish wind had blown the finish line banner down on the Warandelaan. Defilippis was the superior sprinter, and launched his final burst to where a white line was painted, at the beginning of the grandstand. But there was a man waving a dark flag at its end, and another thin mark daubed on the ground. As the Italian sat up, Simpson kept accelerating and crossed this second line first. In the finishing photograph, you can tell that Simpson knows exactly what he is achieving: Britain's first Classic since Arthur Linton won the 1896 Bordeaux-Paris.

Post-race, Defilippis screamed blue murder. "It's a scandal, I was robbed", the Italian champion said. "We could do that sprint again ten times and I'd beat Simpson ten times." His Carpano team manager Vincenzo Giacotto prepared a protest, at both the lack of the banner and lack of an opportunity to inform the racers of its absence. It fell on deaf ears. The more established champion only had himself to blame for such an amateurish mistake. Simpson had little sympathy: "We had already passed the finish line once. How can you get it wrong?"

After 31 finishes in Wetteren, that was the last time the Tour of Flanders ended there. The gone-with-the-wind farce can't have helped, but its position in the denouement owed much to the

friendship between town mayor Jozef du Château and the race's forefather, Karel Van Wijnendaele. After the latter's death in November 1961, the finish moved to Gentbrugge the following year, where Simpson almost made it two Rondes in a row. He followed the decisive break over the Kwaremont with 100 kilometres to go, but focused on the hills prize, finishing the race fifth. Afterwards, he explained to a friend: "I need the money. The primes are very good at the Tour of Flanders, as high as the prize money … I've got my rent to pay, and my wife is due to give birth in two weeks." The following season, he was third behind Noel Foré and Frans Melckenbeek, burned out by working too hard in the decisive break.

It was a mutual love affair between Flanders and Simpson, who spent the last six years of his life in Ghent. Albert Beurick, a young barman who he first met at the 1958 track World Championships in Paris, became a close friend and his biggest supporter. Simpson originally boarded for £5 a week at his establishment, the Café den Engel, in Mariakerke, which became an enclave for fellow British cyclists in the following years, seeking to emulate his feats. A man of the people, Simpson dined in Belgian restaurants, learned some of the local *vlaams* and raised his children there – his daughters Jane and Joanne still live close to Ghent.

In a region where there is a religious fervour for cycling, the locals reciprocated his efforts. "People would come to the door and suddenly there'd be a mound of flowers from people who Tom didn't know [after winning a race]", Barry Hoban said. "That happened in a smaller way with myself … I'd won a couple of stages of the Tour de France, not the Ronde van Vlaanderen. But that's what the people in Belgium are like, they so love the sport."

The message left at Simpson's funeral by the Gentse Velosport club, of which he was a member, showed the depth of their feeling: "You came to Flanders as a small, unknown racing cyclist. You won the heart of all Flemish cycling fans in a very short time. Your charm, your everlasting smile, were two of your secrets. Your fighter's temperament and your great heart made us consider you to be a real Flandrian, one of our own people."

Simpson pips Defilippis for his and Britain's first Monument victory, 1961

LE CHAMPION DU MONDE EST BLESSE A L'ARCADE SOURCILIERE.

SIMPSON A « FAIT LA DECISION » ET SEUL DEFILIPPIS A PRIS SA ROUE. LE MENN, DAEMS, STOLKER, DE HAAN SONT LACHES.

opposé au redoutable finisseur italien

groupe de sept ainsi formé se fut probablement tenu hors de portée du retour de Simpson et Defilippis. Du moins, la chose eut-elle valu la peine d'être vécue.

Van Looy, lorsqu'il reprit la route, comptait deux minutes trente secondes de retard. La partie était irrémédiablement perdue pour lui. Il s'obstina cependant à ne se retirer que trois kilomètres après que son grand rival Van Steenbergen dût lui-même abandonner.

Un Van Steenbergen, trahi nous dit-on par son guidon avant le ravitaillement, mais qui à ce moment déjà ne paraissait plus devoir être en mesure de figurer dans la phase finale.

Van Looy, malchanceux, n'aura donc pu s'offrir qu'une satisfaction d'amour-propre.

CAMILLE LE MENN TRES BON

Si nous avons parfois marqué certaines réticences avec lui, nous ne pouvons que nous incliner quand il se montre aussi remarquable qu'il le fût dans la montée de Kwaremont. Et nous le suivrons de très près dans le prochain Paris-Roubaix.

C'est donc l'ardent Camille Le Menn excellent déjà dans Paris-Nice, qui se classe premier français. Mais « Popof » Graczyk a sauvé l'honneur en prenant sa revanche dans le sprint pour la septième place sur De Cabooter, qui lui avait ravi la victoire l'an dernier.

Poulidor, longtemps discret, essaya vainement de contre-attaquer dans la montée de Valkenberg. Nous aurions aimé le voir plus audacieux, mais ne soyons cependant pas trop exigeant : une fois de plus, il a affiché une grande régularité.

Everaert fut souvent remarqué. Il lui manqua peu de chose en somme pour terminer mieux encore.

Quant à Mahé, on ne sait comment il s'arrange, connaissant une condition aussi parfaite, pour rater aussi régulièrement le « bon wagon » !

Le classement

1. Tom Simpson (St-Raphaël-Gitane), les 255 km en 6 h. 22' ; 2. Defilippis, à 1/4 de roue ; 3. De Haan, 6 h. 22' 11" ; 4. Daems, 6 h. 22' 14" ; 5. Stolker, 6 h. 22' 55' ; 6. Camille Le Menn, 6 h. 22' 59" ; 7. Graczyk, 6 h. 23" ; 8. De Cabooter ; 9. Van Geneunden ; 10. F. Schoubben ; 11. Dewolf ; 12. De Roo ; 13. Foré ; 14. G. De Smet ; 15. Troonbeck... ; 17. Poulidor... ; 22. Everaert, m.t... ; 45. Valdois... ; 47. Cazala.

SIMPSON A DEPLOYE TOUTE SON ENERGIE POUR GAGNER CE SPRINT DEVANT DEFILIPPIS.

Poulidor, toujours leader du Super-Prestige Pernod

Le succès de l'Anglais Tom Simpson (St-Raphaël-Géminiani) dans le Tour de Flandres lui vaut de prendre la deuxième place au Super-Prestige Pernod Arc-en-Ciel, dont le leader reste le Français Poulidor (Mercier-B.P.), qui totalise 80 points. Le classement du Super-Prestige Pernod Arc-en-Ciel est le suivant :

1. Raymond Poulidor (France), 80 pts ; 2. Tom Simpson (Grande-Bretagne), 60 pts ; 3. ex æquo : Rik Van Looy (Belgique) et Nino Defilippis (Italie), 45 pts ; 5. Joannes de Haan (Hollande), 41 pts ; 6. Fernand Picot, 40 pts ; 7. Rino Benedetti, 35 pts ; 8. Edouard Delberghe (France), 30 pts ; 9. ex æquo : Dino Bruni (Italie) et Emile Daems (Belgique), 25 pts.

La prochaine épreuve ayant une influence sur le Super-Prestige Pernod sera Paris-Roubaix le 9 avril.

9

91

1961 PARIS-ROUBAIX: Spectators look on as Simpson waits for a wheel after a badly timed puncture

1961 TOUR DE FRANCE: Not for the first time, Simpson has to visit the doctor's car for some post-crash attention

1961 PARIS-ROUBAIX: Riding at the front and leading 1959 Paris-Roubaix runner-up Gilbert Desmet

1963 Bordeaux-Paris

Bordeaux-Paris was a fiendish *fin de siècle* test devised in cycle racing's infancy to demonstrate what man could do. The 557-kilometre event between two great French metropolitan hubs took the first winner, British amateur George Pilkington Mills, 26 and a half hours in 1890. Winning times had nearly halved by the Sixties, and this unique challenge had become an outdated antique, albeit one which held a great sentimental attachment, akin to an ornate gramophone in a living room full of mod-cons.

Simpson approached his debut appearance at this institution hungry from a spring of near misses. He had helped team-mate Emile Daems to Paris-Roubaix victory, and his lone breakaway was snuffed out in the closing kilometres of Liège-Bastogne-Liège, leading to a tearful phone call with his wife Helen. He wanted dearly to win, and he made sure he was ready: you didn't just rock-up to Bordeaux-Paris on a whim. As the start city's great philosopher Montaigne wrote, "*Qui craint de souffrir souffre déjà de ce qu'il craint*" – "he who fears he shall suffer, already suffers what he fears." Simpson prepared assiduously in Ghent, and left five days before the start, hours after witnessing the birth of his second daughter, Joanne. However, the week was not entirely blessed by good timing. Hours before the race, Simpson woke up from a nap and fainted. He put it down to nervous tension.

Fifteen men took to the start on Bordeaux's famous Pont de Pierre, clad in bulbous ski gloves, eye shields and woolly hats. An early challenge of this marathon race was avoiding mishap between the 2am start and sunrise, as mind and body sought sleep. Through the rest of the night, the competitors went along at 20mph in a blackness intermittently broken by the light projected from following press cars and motorcycles. Simpson stayed unusually quiet for all but the race's final moments, saving his words as if each one was

Riding away from the rest, under the expert eye of derny pacer Fernand Wambst

a precious acceleration. "Peter Post was very chatty all night", the Briton said of the Dutch favourite afterwards. "He'd have done better to keep quiet."

Riding from the pitch black of the Bordeaux night to Paris, the "city of light", the racers took in a dozen départements and all manner of life and class on the roadside: dreary-eyed dressing gown wearers, ruddy country *paysans* in their berets and packed Parisian crowds in their Sunday best. The *Miroir des Sports* journalist Paul Hamelle likened the event to "a drama of 100

different acts … it is the greatest race there is, was or ever will be."

For the wannabe winner, Bordeaux-Paris was an exercise in patience, judgement, endurance, concentration and suffering. The race's demanding distance resulted in a few quirks: Simpson used concentrated food for sustenance during the race, similar to the kind given to post-operative patients in hospitals at the time. The riders stopped as a group to change kit at Poitiers, then picked up derny motorbikes to pace them at Châtellerault after 259 kilometres. These orange motorised

All smiles entering the Parc des Princes on the wheel of Wambst

machines, which buzzed like chainsaws, were a defining feature of Bordeaux-Paris and heralded the start of the race proper.

They were usually manned by experienced former racers with tactical savvy: Simpson's Belgian pacer Fernand Wambst was analysing both his own charge and his rivals, planning when to make their move. He had first spotted Simpson's smoothness behind a derny while training his then-team-mate Jo de Haan for *le Derby de la route*, as the French nicknamed the race, a couple of years before.

Despite his ease behind the derny, every rider experiences a debilitating patch in Bordeaux-Paris. Simpson's low came in the two hours after meeting the pacers, with the race's speed still steady. At this point, the Dutch pair of Piet Rentmeester and Bas Maliepaard had established an eight-minute lead. With 150 kilometres still to go, at Cloyes-sur-le-Loir, Wambst asked Simpson if he was okay. He nodded and they upped the pace in pursuit. Nobody could follow. It took Simpson just an hour to cross the eight-minute gap to the leaders. Passing by Chartres and its grand Gothic cathedral

Simpson's win was emphatic. By the finish line, he had five minutes in hand over second placed Piet Rentmeester

Peugeot team
manager Gaston Plaud
(left) congratulates
Simpson in the track
centre at the Parc
de Princes after the
15-hour epic

signified the beginning of the race's endgame and the approach to the Chevreuse valley, its lush, leg-hurting hills transforming into decisive action points after 14 hours of racing. On the drag at Dourdan, 65 kilometres from Paris, Simpson rode away. As his rivals toiled, the Peugeot champion had energy left to burn.

However, maintaining focus during such a long race was another test. A few kilometres down the road, there was a nerve-wracking moment as Simpson touched Wambst's derny fender with his front wheel, but stayed upright. His form on the bike was still majestic: according to one report, the legendary British cycling journalist Jock Wadley was reduced to tears by the ease with which Simpson climbed the hill at Saint-Rémy-lès-Chevreuse.

Five minutes up on closest challenger Piet Rentmeester, it was Simpson's turn to cry at the finish in the Parc des Princes after an *échappée magistrale*. "I feel that I've revenged myself on everybody. I had the idea that everybody was riding to cut me out, which is why victory is so sweet now", he told *L'Equipe*. These were the last halcyon days for Bordeaux-Paris, with Jacques Anquetil and Jan Janssen soon joining Simpson in its annals before this fabulous folly of a bike race met a gradual decline.

Meanwhile, there was one more successful race against time for Simpson: getting back to Ghent in time to see his wife and newborn daughter. They kept the hospital doors open for him after visiting hours and he presented his winner's bouquet of flowers to Helen.

The triumph set Simpson on the path to numerous lucrative criterium contracts, a financial buffer which contributed to his decision to skip the 1963 Tour de France. But Simpson was soon frustrated by more near misses. He sprinted to second place at Paris-Tours on the way to a runner-up placing in the Super Prestige Pernod, the season-long competition based on results in top races throughout the year. When consolatory journalists afterwards reminded him of his rousing victory at the Parc des Princes four months earlier, he quipped: "But you didn't see, I finished second again – behind my pacer."

1963 PARIS-BRUSSELS: Eventual winner
and wily French classics ace Jean
Stablinski leads Tom across the Brussels cobbles

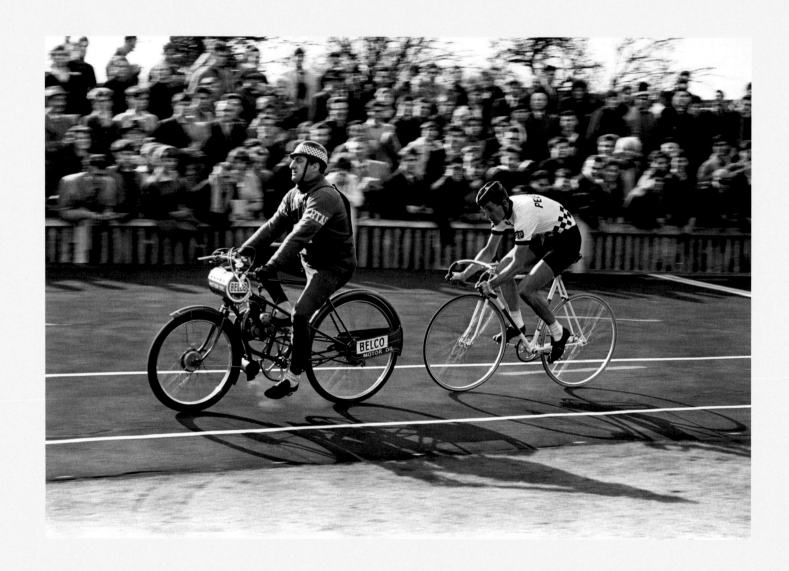

1963 HERNE HILL: Simpson draws a capacity crowd for the Good Friday Meeting. Photograph by Gerry Cranham

1963 GHENT-WEVELGEM: Benoni Beheyt
beats Simpson to the line, with
Michel Van Aerde on his shoulder. It was so close
to call that the Briton demanded to see the photo
finish afterwards

1964 Milan-Sanremo

Milan-Sanremo is a lottery, so the cliché goes. Except it's wrong, simplistic, loser's talk. The word implies everyone has the same chance, and that's not true of any cycling race. It is better to call it cycling's most inclusive Classic, its finely balanced, unusually long route letting sprinters, puncheurs, rouleurs and Grand Tour contenders dare to dream. There are many things a rider can do to improve his probability of winning this supposed lottery: buy his team-mates' tickets, for starters. The reliability of Simpson's Peugeot comrades was as chequered as their legendary jerseys. "It's very rare when I can get 100 or even 50 per cent support from the Peugeot team. Most of them are young fellows who won't sacrifice themselves, but who want someone else to help them", Simpson says in the film *Something To Aim At.*

Ad hoc teamwork rarely existed: a leader paid his team-mates to lend a hand or put up with their independent racing. Sometimes, there were more complex external factors at work too. Before Simpson's emergence, Brian Robinson had Britain's only Monument podium result, finishing third in the 1957 Milan-Sanremo. However, his ambitions were compromised in the finale, as he obliged team manager Raymond Louviot's pre-race request to help rival and fellow breakaway Miguel Poblet, because his Saint-Raphaël team was courting him. So before the 1964 race, Simpson signed a contract with the other seven Peugeot riders, stipulating his prize money would go to them if he won.

It was well worth getting them on side. Milan-Sanremo was a free-for-all, with dozens of Italian independent riders thrown into the mix, leading to a field of 232 riders haring *prestissimo* out of Milan and south into the Piedmont valley. Simpson had been surprised

Peugeot directeur sportif Gaston Plaud cracks the jokes as Tom and the team tuck into beer and a platter of sandwiches, 1964

Raymond Poulidor and Simpson force the issue on the Poggio, Willy Bocklandt and Vincenzo Meco are dropped, 1964

by this early charge on his 1960 debut. "I was completely unprepared for such early speed and in no time at all, I was right at the back of the field … it took me 80 kilometres of really hard riding to reach the leaders", he recalled in the magazine *Cycling*. The dense bunch and narrow Italian streets made it a claustrophobic Classic; after winning the race in 1964, Simpson found four bent spokes in his wheels. In what he called "the most dangerous race in the world", attacking was never a bad choice.

Picking the right moment at Milan-Sanremo is akin to playing sporting Russian roulette with a gun where all but one chamber is loaded. Go too early in the 288-kilometre race and a favourite might be shooting himself in the foot, as Simpson did in 1960. His fear fuelled a fatal, premature lone attack on the race's earliest climb, the Turchino. His team manager Louviot tore strips off him afterwards for losing out on millions of lire for the team. Lesson learned. Once the race hit the Italian Riviera, the short Ligurian *capi* hills, as punchy as their names – Mele, Cervo, Berta – provided an opportunity for more moves. But wait too long to attack, and a contender might be condemned to sprint for the lesser placings or be left powerless to lead a chase if a team-mate was up the road. With a sizeable bunch on sinuous roads, there was always the risk of being stuck behind a crash too. All told, at Milan-Sanremo, there is a powerful need to trust one's instinct, which suited Simpson the gambler. "I love to see how far I can go, what risks I can get away with, which is why I always try the unexpected", he said in one interview.

He ignited the race on the Capo Berta, 30 kilometres from Sanremo, bringing Willy Bocklandt, Vincenzo Meco and Raymond Poulidor with him. They were no chumps: the Belgian would claim Liège-Bastogne-Liège a month later, Meco was a Giro d'Italia stage winner and Poulidor had won Milan-Sanremo in 1961. The group had a minute's lead by the foot of the Poggio, the race's final climb and kingmaker. Poulidor launched several accelerations there, and Simpson replied over a number of seconds, rather than pushing himself into the red immediately. This might have been down to his gearing too: he later claimed that he rode the finale with only three sprockets working on his freewheel, due to a plastic bag jamming in them.

"These people are going to crush me!" First across the line on the Via Roma means plenty of attention for the winner

After descending together into Sanremo, the duo started their sprint side-by-side, but as Simpson wound up his 53×14 top gear, the Frenchman melted away. "He was very intelligent as a rider, he had a way of racing that was quite remarkable", Poulidor says. "We also said that Simpson sold a lot of races. It's true. But we did a regular sprint that day." The passionate Italian crowd in Sanremo was too exuberant for this *capo* of the *capi*. Finding his Peugeot soigneur Gus Naessens in the throng, Simpson told him: "Take me to a hotel, quick, these people are going to crush me!" After being cleaned with cologne, he ended up in room 223 of the Hotel Plaza with journalist Gigi Boccaini, who had followed him.

Boccaini retold their discussion the following day in the pages of *La Stampa*. In his account, Simpson got hold of a bar of soap, a litre of cold milk and held court, telling the waiter to get his guest whatever he wanted. "He was in the bath, naked as a buckworm", Boccaini writes. "And he was having fun, behaving like an old-fashioned gentleman who welcomes you to his castle." Simpson gave his opinion of the race, explained his route to the top and some of the curiosities of the British cycling scene, including a mention of the road racing rule of stopping at traffic lights. The encounter is impossible to imagine now in a time of public relations mollycoddling. The Italian press of Simpson's era, who always liked to exaggerate his Britishness, subsequently suggested that he would be received at Buckingham Palace by the Queen. It's a far-fetched suggestion, but perhaps even Her Majesty might have been curious to hear how Simpson had turned this so-called lottery into a sure thing.

1964 TOUR DE FRANCE: Breaking away
on his own again

1964 **TOUR DE FRANCE:** Mechanical trouble lost Simpson precious time on stage 8 from Thonon-les-Bains to Briançon

1964 TOUR DE FRANCE: The race-
ending time-trial to Paris.
Tom would finish the race 14th overall

1964 PARIS-ROUBAIX: Up and riding after
a crash in "the Hell of the North"

1965 Tour of Lombardy

Arriving in Milan on the eve of the Tour of Lombardy, the international peloton could have been forgiven for thinking the period's British Invasion had been all too literal. The Union Jack was flying in Piazza Duomo, London buses and bobbies were doing the rounds in the centre, and the city was appropriately shrouded in a pea souper. It was Settimana Britannica – British Week – in Italy's industrial hub, a thin excuse to celebrate the increased trade and cordiality between the two countries. Festivities opened with a Military Tattoo at the Palazzo dello Sport playing a mix of military songs and Beatles hits to a half-full audience, due to the high ticket prices. Prince Philip was there too, presenting medals at an Inter Milan versus Chelsea friendly and watching Nureyev's twinkling toes at the Scala. There was another uninhibited, willowy British icon in town: Tom Simpson. Naturally, the Italian press said his victory at the Tour of Lombardy was fated.

Simpson didn't just want to win, he *needed* to win. Within weeks of his World Championship triumph in San Sebastian, his rainbow jersey was sullied by scandal. Having accepted a sizeable offer from *The People* tabloid to dish some tales from the milieu, his first-person articles caused a storm. The mild revelations included offering £1,100 to rival Shay Elliott for help at the 1963 World Championships, taking a payment of £500 to help another rider and his use of medical "tonics": indecorous behaviour perhaps, yet common for the sport at the time. When the story crossed the Channel, several European newspapers had a field day. Peugeot held Simpson back from the Grand Prix du Parisien and threatened to fire him. Jacques Anquetil and Jean Stablinski, aristocrats of the French scene, had an altercation with him about the articles at one criterium. The British Cycling Federation and UCI demanded

explanations too, though its governing body's secretary showed understanding. "He had the courage to speak up", René Chesal told *L'Equipe*. "In doing so, he has exposed the hypocrisy and the feudal system which has existed for so long among the pros."

Despite the controversy, Simpson's sense of humour was still intact. At the Tour of Lombardy pre-race meeting in Milan's modernist Pirelli Tower, he informed journalists he had "the world champion of all colds" and pretended to write more scurrilous revelations on a piece of paper before screwing it up and chucking it at a commissaire. The clowning disguised Simpson's burning desire to win a classic where he had unfinished business. Twelve months earlier, Gianni Motta, the blue-eyed, blonde-haired *bambino* of the Molteni team, had escaped with him and dropped him 20 kilometres from Como. Motta

won; Simpson endured the mother of all bonks, finishing nine minutes behind him. The journalist Roger St Pierre claimed he had to undo Simpson's shoelaces for him in the changing rooms, such was his fatigue. The misty shores of Lake Como and the route's six steep, wooded climbs around it made a striking arena for Simpson's revenge. "It's the most beautiful race in the world", Motta tells me.

Italo Zilioli made the running over the Muro di Sormano, a climb so severe that riders would often end up pushing their bikes up the steepest reaches. Afterwards, Simpson escaped on the descent of the second climb, the Ghisallo, and helped to form the dozen-strong lead group. "You didn't know what Tom was going to do. He would attack going uphill, downhill, on a Classic. He'd go from the start or he'd play it cagey and go at the finish. You couldn't just rest happy when Tom was

On the climb of the Ghisallo with Renzo Fontona (left), Roberto Poggiali (right) and Gianni Motta behind

there. He would have a go over and over again", Barry Hoban says.

The pace and regular climbs eventually whittled the contenders down to Simpson, Motta, two-time Giro winner Imerio Massignan and Roberto Poggiali on the Intelvi, 60 kilometres from the finish. Then on the last climb, the San Fermo della Battiglia, there were two: the same protagonists as 1964. But this time, the outcome was reversed. "Tom said to me 'Gianni, I can't do any more work', and I continued to pull and pull", Motta recalls. "However, when we got to the final climb, he went for it. You could say he was a bit craftier, but that's part of the game. Everyone does whatever they can."

Caught by his rivals late on, the Italian was in tears after the race, but is at pains to stress Simpson's goodness. "It didn't change our friendship. Tom was a brilliant man, not false. He wanted good for everyone."

Simpson rode into the finish at Como's Stadio Sinigaglia, three minutes and 11 seconds ahead of the chasers. It was the race's most emphatic winning margin since the great Fausto Coppi scattered all and sundry in 1948. And just like his childhood hero, Simpson won from the front and thoroughly outclassed his rivals.

"To forget this [*People*] story, I didn't have a choice of means: to win a grand classic. Now, I am happy because I've proven that I know how to respect the jersey like a world champion should", Simpson said afterwards.

Taking the race by the scruff of the neck for 200 kilometres epitomised his exciting philosophy of cycling. When it came to enterprising tactics and outlasting everyone else, there were few better than Simpson. The Tour of Lombardy turned out to be his final significant one-day race victory. He didn't know it then, but the best had been left till last.

At Como's Stadio Sinigaglia, Simpson wins alone

1965 PARIS-TOURS: World
champion on the warpath

1965 TOUR DE FRANCE: After a crash on the descent of the Col d'Aubisque, stage 9. Road rash, a gashed elbow and hand made for a difficult next few stages

1965 BORDEAUX-PARIS: Getting changed
during the marathon one-day race

1965 BRUSSELS SIX-DAY: Simpson
and tea-drinking partner Peter
Post went on to win overall

124

Chapter Six

FROM MINOR TO MAJOR

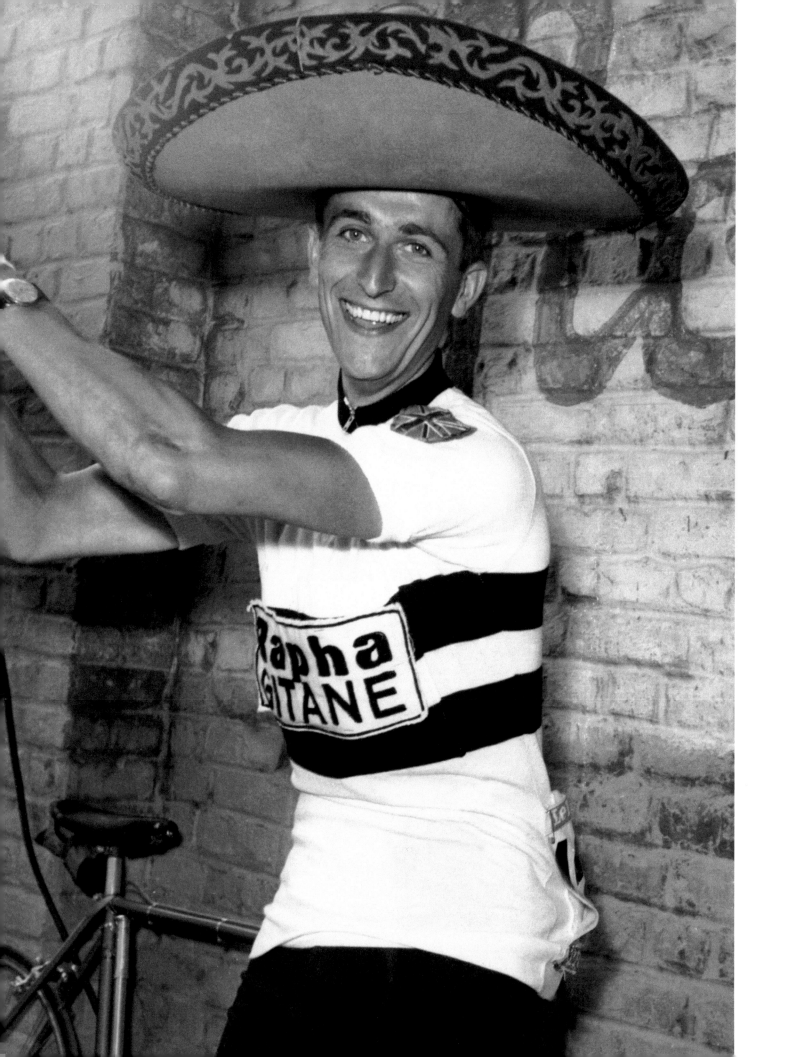

Winning top bike races is one thing, winning the hearts of the public is quite another. Different people are moved by different traits. It can be a champion with emphatic shows of strengths, the intelligence of a crafty winner or the heart and perseverance of an underdog. Most commonly, we unite in acclaiming sporting gold and its few purveyors. When Lionel Messi dribbles past four hapless defenders before chipping the goalkeeper, or Seve Ballesteros used a three-wood to get to the edge of the green from a bunker 220 yards away, we delight in both the mastery and its inconceivability. How on earth did they do that?

There can be joy in a certain relatability too. While Fausto Coppi and Jacques Anquetil were veritable gods, Simpson was a kid from a British mining town who worshipped at their altar like everyone else and came to compete on the same plane. He was not the greatest natural talent or a conjurer of magic, but a man who maintained an emotional transparency on and off the bike. His heart-on-the-sleeve suffering was clear to see and his outlook on life was humble.

"I like to be liked and to be accepted by other people, not because I might be somebody special, but just to be able to talk and joke with folk and share a laugh", he wrote in his autobiography *Cycling is my Life*. During his career, Simpson won the popularity he sought, helped by his sparkling personality and the creation of an exceptional persona. Simpson's British upbringing, and the backward nature of cycle racing in his homeland, put him at a disadvantage when it came to the complexities of Continental racing, but it was a useful quirk for column inches. In his early years abroad, he became a prism through which British stereotypes were played in the press. After his 1961 Tour of Flanders victory, his manager Daniel Dousset had the idea of dressing Simpson as an English gentleman in the image of Major William Marmaduke Thompson, a popular literary creation of French writer Pierre Daninos. His smash hit book, *Les Carnets du Major Thompson*, included witty observations on French and British life through the eyes of this permanently befuddled retired army officer.

Thompson is an Oxford-educated gentleman with a white moustache and prominent teeth, who was fond of cups of tea and puffing on his pipe – a walking, talking, bowler hat-bedecked British caricature. Naturally, he is perplexed by encountering the Tour de France, describing the scene as "two male individuals, gracelessly swaying on their bicycles, festooned with inner tubes and tyres and clad in glaring jerseys and exiguous shorts, covered with mud, altogether rather a shocking sight … getting to Paris as quickly as possible by the slowest roads, which seemed strange to me."

On a subsequent photo shoot in Paris with *Miroir-Sprint*, Simpson went full-on Major, clad in bowler hat and sharp suit. He completed the look with a briefcase, umbrella, cup of tea and a copy of *The Times* spread in front of him on a café table. Even his name, a portmanteau of the eccentric major's surname, fitted the bill. His get-up caused a minor sensation: the persona of Major Tom was born.

Simpson was far happier to ham it up for publicity than his British predecessor Brian Robinson. At the 1960 Tour de France, he embarked on a campaign of wearing a different hat every morning, which annoyed the fastidious race officials. Over the years, he donned berets, sombreros, a tri-corner, a Yorkshire cap and a fireman's helmet. "I've even seen him pick up a ukulele and play at being George Formby – with his bowler hat on. And the press loved it", says Alan Ramsbottom, his Peugeot team-mate.

French journalists happily took the British angle and ran with it, describing him in his early years as "having aristocratic legs" and "hanging an Eton tie on his handlebars". Simpson's modest upbringing in Harworth was nowhere near such noble pleasures, but it probably read well to the average Frenchman. Besides, the exaggerated caricature exists both sides of the Channel: when was the last time you saw a moustachioed,

Mad hatter: Simpson rocks a sombrero, 1960 Tour de France

127

Major Tom in the yellow jersey at his hotel in Luchon, 1962 Tour de France

beret-wearing Frenchman with a string of onions round his neck?

For all this apparent urbanity, Simpson occasionally got into slapstick scrapes more befitting his cartoon namesake, Homer. One night in Auxerre after a 1964 Paris-Nice stage, his warming embrocation dramatically burst into life as he was about to go to sleep, leading to a comical scene where his soigneur had to douse his burning legs with a mix of vinegar and water. The next season, he contrived to close a car door on his foot before the Tour of Belgium, and suffered a broken leg while skiing in Saint-Gervais that winter. Even afterwards, his impulsiveness was irrepressible: according to Vin Denson, he went riding down the towpath with his leg in plaster to keep everything ticking over.

There is a movie-star magnetism to Simpson in front of the camera. Almost unfailingly smiling into the lens – off the bike, at least – he exudes warmth. Armed with boyish good looks and a cheeky character, Simpson caught the attention of the press and the public. "He was popular with the ladies. There was a gang of groupies that used

Messing about with
the photographers
before stage 21,
1960 Tour de France

to follow the event, they went with the managers. There were a lot of women followers, hangers-on", Ramsbottom says.

While his taciturn Peugeot team-mate Roger Pingeon, for instance, kept his room number secret on Tour and rigorously controlled the length of each interview, Simpson understood the need to be generous in his dealings. In a 1967 interview with *Cycling*, he says that the object of the professional cyclist is "to secure as much publicity as possible for his sponsors: he is an entertainer, a publicity agent and a sportsman all rolled into one, in that order. It is up to the rider to get all the publicity he can: publicity for the cyclist means publicity for the sponsor and that means that people get to know of his products and buy them, whether they be wines, refrigerators or washing machines."

Simpson's bowler hat proved an astute device for gaining attention, an unmistakable byword for both his nationality and comedy. While the headwear's roots lie in the Victorian working class, Charlie Chaplin and Stan Laurel wore it to good effect too. "Often warming up before a

129

criterium, he'd pop that on to amuse the crowd. He liked to be liked, to clown about and give the spectators a lot back", Vin Denson recalls. Simpson rarely donned his bowler after early 1963, concerned that it was jinxing his results, but it nevertheless became the emblematic prop among the many he owned.

"He used to have a little bag [of hats] in his case. He had a clown's one and a policeman's bobby helmet on an elastic band, which he'd put over his crash hat", Vin Denson says, recalling one devil-take-the-hindmost track race. "He had a whistle, he'd blow at the person who was going to get eliminated, flash up the banking and nip past him. He did all his track racing from the back."

The track scene was not just a decent winter payday that suited his versatility, but also a perfect arena, akin to a sporting big top, for his antics. Simpson raced Six Day events extensively between 1963 and 1967; fellow British competitor Norman Hill recalls Simpson's shenanigans at one Antwerp Six. "Artists-singers, jazz musicians and showbiz personalities would be hired as entertainment between races. On this occasion, a circus troupe was on hand", he says. "Somehow, Tom got involved and opened the monkey cage. The monkey scrambled up into the rafters just under the roof and wouldn't come down for several hours. In fact, by the time the circus troupe got it down to eat, it was the early hours! During that time, the race was stopped and the track director, Theo Balemans, was furious at Tom. Mind you, the beer flowed, spectators got drunk and the riders, soigneurs and runners were happy – Six Days back then were a 100-kilometre Madison every night and riding from noon to five in the morning."

Larking about with two majorettes in Athis-Mons, 1967 Paris-Nice

Simpson formed part of a long tradition of racers making people laugh while they suffered, which includes his old team-mate Roger Hassenforder, later rival Gerben Karstens and modern-day cult hero Jens Voigt. All developed a fan base built on outstanding charisma as well as impressive results. Nowadays, Simpson's actions might be dissected as part of a calculated construction of his personal brand. But the light-heartedness was a gentle extension of his vivacious character rather than posturing. "I am never happier than when I am making people laugh", he wrote in *Cycling* in 1961. And Simpson would do anything for some fun: riding a penny farthing at one Herne Hill meet, sledging with Saint-Raphaël team-mates at the ski resort of Peïra-Cava during early-season races and hamming it up on an accordion before a Tour de France stage.

A bon vivant who liked to drive fast and laugh hard, Simpson crammed as many adventures and memorable moments into his 29 and a half years as some people would do in their entire lives. The film director Shane Meadows, who has spoken of his intention to produce a Simpson biopic, described him as "like Keith Moon on a bike … the first rock 'n' roll cyclist", to *Shortlist*. Simpson's character feeds the myth too. Several stories are excavated during the research and interview process which nobody can corroborate. The pick of the lot has Simpson spending several nights performing on stage with Coco the Clown at the Cirque d'Hiver in Paris one winter; another suggests he turned up unannounced at a Belgian hospital for hydrocephalic children with three bags of sweets for them. Unsure whether they're true or not, Helen Hoban concedes, "it's the kind of thing he'd do."

Playing to the crowd on a donkey before stage 16 of the 1964 Tour de France

1965 GP AMITIÉ
PUTEAUX
CRITERIUM: The World
Champion is in high
demand

1964 HERNE HILL:
Signing an autograph
for a young fan

Interviews were once a very relaxed affair. With René de Latour, the Sporting Cyclist correspondent, in Brussels at stage 2, 1960 Tour de France

For all the tomfoolery, Simpson was dead serious about his cycling career and recognised that without significant results, the comedy might become his calling card, akin to fellow rider Roger Hassenforder, who gained the nickname "The Clown". There was nothing particularly wrong with that, but he had higher ambitions. Simpson always tried to finish highly at criteriums, alongside the larking: "Thus the public, who would come to the meeting prepared to see an entertainer, would also see and remember me as a good racing cyclist", he explains in *Cycling*. He had an implicit understanding of his role: "A great thing to be remembered by a top racing man is that he is not so much a public idol but rather a friend of the public – someone with whom the man on the street would like to be associated."

So, he blended English humour with heroic racing. It has been suggested that Simpson possessed a superior ability to suffer than most of his peers. In truth, it's an unquantifiable trait that is particularly easy to romanticise after his death on Mont Ventoux. But anecdotally, Simpson's exceptional grit still rises to the surface today. Vin Denson recounts a tale relating to the 1964 Trofeo Baracchi two-up time-trial, where the Briton turned himself inside out to keep up with partner Rudi Altig in the race's second half. "Tom told me [later] 'All my worries and pain had ended, I was drifting along as if I was in a cloud, not really interested in life at all. I'm not kidding Vin, I basically died.' And he saw that everything was so peaceful. When you're that far, and you've drifted away, you're completely void of everything."

Alan Ramsbottom also witnessed how hard Simpson could push himself. "I remember coming into Saint-Étienne in one Paris-Nice. It was the last few miles, it just dragged up and up. Tommy had been riding like a hero. And all of a sudden, I see him going backwards. He lost half an hour in about three miles. He could barely steer his bicycle properly when he got to the finish. He was completely wiped out. He was all right the day after but I've never seen anybody get that bad. Not many riders can do that: I never could."

The Dutch star Jan Janssen felt a kinship with Simpson through his personality, as well as their racing characteristics. "He had a bit of class, but such courage. And I was a bit the same … But he was a stylist, a joy, beautiful on the bike. I wasn't."

Like Simpson, Janssen was also a world champion and a racer who stood out, distinctive in his Roy Orbison-esque shaded sunglasses. He achieved what his friend never managed too: the Audi sitting in his garage, with the number plate "Tour 68", bears testament to the first Dutch Tour de France triumph. In his house on a quiet road by the Belgium-Netherlands border, Janssen is a picture of hard-fought health. After running a successful bicycle business post-cycling, he fought through stomach cancer in 2015. Happily, a shock of white hair grew back after the chemotherapy and this animated raconteur is back riding his bike regularly.

Living only an hour apart in the mid-Sixties, with Simpson based in Ghent and Janssen on the Dutch border, the pair became friends and shared a car to races when it was mutually convenient. One afternoon, they were in a rush, as professional cyclists usually are, driving through the central French city of Châteauroux on the way to a criterium in Limoges.

"Back then, there were no motorways and we were on *routes nationales*. There was a big boulevard that crossed the town. Every 100 metres, there was a red light. Next to our car at one, there was a gendarme on a bicycle. As the light turned green, Tommy suddenly mooned the policeman, who wasn't pleased to say the least. He was screaming 'Stop!' Then we got to another red light, it went green, we were off again. We could hear his whistle behind us, the gendarme on the bike really fought to catch us. But every 100 metres, we had to stop again. By the fifth or sixth set of lights, he was in front of the car", Janssen says, imitating the red-faced officer draping himself over the bonnet.

Janssen and Simpson were hauled off to the local police station. It seemed that they wouldn't be leaving Châteauroux before dark. But then, Simpson went off on such a stirring and emotive tale about the nomadic adventures of the professional cyclist that the gendarme ended up feeling sorry for them and let the pair go with a telling-off. "The gendarme said to us, it's not honest, you mustn't do that to a policeman. It cost us a couple of hours and a hefty fine – not to mention arriving in Limoges at midnight", Janssen says. Simpson gave the officer a signed photograph to sweeten the deal.

Outside in the garden, Janssen's two dogs jump and bark at one other, like something out of a Gainsborough painting. The Dutchman doesn't pay attention, lost in another recollection of his friend. "Occasionally, Tommy was annoying. When it was rolling along at 30 kilometres an hour – paf!" He slaps his hand down on the dark wooden dining table. "He'd attack. Oh, leave us alone! There's still 150 kilometres to go, pipe down. But often, he wanted war."

Janssen's face creases into a frown. He rubs his temple and makes a noise like a growling throttle. "Even in the feed zones. It's not the law, but it's not polite. Musettes were up in the air, there was panic and crashes. It was Simpson acting like a jerk. It didn't happen often, occasionally I was angry at him. I'd say to him in his native English: 'you fucking cunt!'" Janssen says, with a laugh. Simpson was the loveable rogue and his charm regularly mended any lingering discord. "There were often many teams, five or six, in the same

Bird on the wire

Even with a broken leg, the show must go on: going over race contracts with his manager Daniel Dousset, 1966

"It was the golden age of cycling", Janssen says. "Now, there are still stars but I notice there is not as much friendship between riders … During the races back then, we had enemies, the knife was on the table. But outside them, we'd drink wine or beer and we sang together. How super, *quelle belle époque*. That doesn't exist anymore."

Simpson's occasional defiance of unwritten peloton rules, like attacking in the feed zone, was a reason why he earned a reputation as a bit of a rebel, though he didn't particularly consider himself one. "[It's] because I'm outspoken. I've got my own ideas and I always try to stick by them", he says in the film *Something To Aim At*. The 1965 affair with *The People* newspaper, where he was punished for publicly expressing grubby truths about the peloton, exemplified that. The allegations scuppered Peugeot's intended "Gentleman Tom" publicity campaign, although there was a certain irony that he was still getting them column inches, albeit for the wrong reasons. The fee offered by the newspaper had been a big motivation for the articles, but he ended up donating it to the charity fund of the professional cyclists' union.

hotel together every evening. Each had their own table. And at a certain moment, Tommy walked into the restaurant like a gentleman – with a bowler hat, cane and in costume", Janssen says, miming an aristocratic entrance. "He was like a Lord in England, and the rest of us were in tracksuits. Everyone saw that, laughed and the things he had done in the race were forgotten."

In an era of greater contact and camaraderie between riders, Simpson was well-liked by his peers, even those who didn't speak the same language. After a dramatic finish to the 1967 Tour of Spain in Bilbao, when saboteurs left tin-tacks and oil on the road, a host of riders travelled by train to Paris to race the Polymultiplée in the outlying town of Chanteloup. But Simpson missed the initial connection and caught a taxi over the border to intercept it in Bayonne. Once on board, despite knowing no Spanish, he had the climber Julio Jimenez in stitches, explaining his palaver through mime and gesture, and how he felt incapable of putting one pedal in front of the other at the next day's event.

When it came to making money, Simpson didn't mess around. He would occasionally try to smuggle items across borders to avoid paying import duty. While moving to Ghent, he was stopped by customs officials, trying to finagle a radio through. His Peugeot team-mate Henri Duez recalls a far more potent cargo. "Tom told the hunters on the team that he knew someone at the famous weapons factory of Herstal [in Belgium] and could get hold of a gun at a good price", he says. "I was the buyer. I remember the evening of the 1963 Paris–Brussels, where he came second behind Jean Stablinski. He crossed the border afterwards with three guns on the back seat, including mine."

"The customs officials, having seen cycling kit, casquettes and photographs on the car seats, quickly recognised it was Simpson, whose exploits they had been following on the radio. So there was an autograph-signing session and the guns got through undetected. The car hadn't even been

searched." Over 50 years later, Duez still has the elegant, wooden-handled weapon on display in his hallway.

Despite showing his streetwise nature, Simpson could be naïve in other scenarios, especially in his early days on the Continent. It only took him a few hours abroad before getting fleeced, fittingly on April Fools' Day 1959. Stumbling around with two bicycles, two suitcases and a haversack, this innocent abroad was charged an excessive 40 francs taxi fare to get between two train stations in Paris. Years later, he also discovered that Vins Santa Rosa, the Breton company that backed him during his whistle-stop rise in 1959, had paid him well below the odds. In his autobiography, Simpson acknowledged his gullibility: "I have had and still have too much confidence in people. I'm the most easily duped person in the world."

His good faith led to problems. In 1965, he invested in the construction of two apartment blocks in the east Ghent suburb of Sint-Amandsberg. According to Barry Hoban, as construction costs rocketed, the builders made necessary cuts to the original plans. Yet, taking bad advice from the notary who oversaw the transaction, Simpson still agreed to advertise the apartments alongside the original layouts, when they ought to have been sold as seen. The various owners later formed a syndicate and took the Hobans to court when they realised the error. "Tom believed in people. He believed they would do right. And they didn't", Barry Hoban says.

Several team-mates attest to his good-heartedness. André Desvages, a first-year professional with Peugeot in 1967, was stunned at how much this champion cared about him. "When I had Belgian races, he came to welcome me at the train station in Ghent or found me a hotel", he says. At Paris-Nice, Simpson gave him advice about getting in the breakaway and was delighted to later discover that Desvages had won the stage.

Vin Denson remembers another act of kindness. "[My wife] Vi and I opened a café in Ghent, I had all these sporting kits in a net [on the ceiling], football shirts, bike riders' jerseys,

1967 TOUR DE FRANCE: Simpson picks a
daisy for the cameras, stage 2, Saint-Malo

1966 TOUR DE FRANCE: Tom's attempts to play the accordion are music to the ears of Louis Rostollan (left) and Raymond Mastrotto (right)

How to look good
on a bike

Anquetil's one", he says. "The only thing missing was a yellow jersey. Tom came into the pub one night with Helen, we were having a chat and a meal. He said 'hang on, I've got something for you.' And he pulled out the yellow jersey [from 1962] and said: 'I'm keeping one for my daughters and here's one for you.'"

With so many dimensions to his character, Simpson left the Major Tom persona behind and blew away the dusty stereotypes of the composed, traditional Englishman. He could play the Lord and the larrikin, the committed star and the clown, the underdog and the champion, be cold-blooded or clumsy, stoic or lachrymose. Take your pick from times he cried: at the 1956 Olympic closing ceremony, on his 1962 Tour lap of honour and his abandon three years later, after losing Liège-Bastogne-Liège, winning Bordeaux-Paris in 1963 and a narrow defeat in the 1964 World Championships. Simpson became far more cosmopolitan than the Major he had started out mimicking. The journalist Jean Bobet described him as "the first English Continental rider … ambitious like a Frenchman, selfish like a Spaniard, industrious like a German, talkative like an Italian and versatile like a Fleming." It was this everyman appeal which helped him to win over such a broad cross-section of people. While his world-beating results got him an invitation to the proverbial party of top riders, his magnetic personality made him the life and soul of it, and helps to sustain his memory today. As Larkin wrote, "what will survive of us is love" and there's an abundance left for Simpson. Vin Denson, Henri Duez and Jan Janssen all use the same words to describe their bond: "We were like brothers."

The anti-hero trait that sticks to Tom Simpson is the one he could never rectify: that of being a cheat, following the discovery of amphetamine pills in his pockets on Mont Ventoux after his death. To most of his peers, that transgression is irrelevant to their perception of Simpson. "Nobody had a bad word to say for him", his old Olympic team-mate Billy Holmes says. "I'm anti-drugs, but I wasn't anti-Tommy. I was never anti-Tommy."

144

Chapter Seven

JE T'AIME, MOI NON PLUS

"*Tom failed many times, but it is because he tries so much so often that his record is so beautiful*"

Raymond Louviot, Simpson's former team manager, 1966

July 5 1962. Tom Simpson sat in his hotel in Saint-Gaudens, recovering from an extraordinary Tour de France stage with toast and jam and his favourite herbal tea, mint and lime blossom. There were cuts and road rash over his body, caused by a crash on the descent of the Col du Tourmalet a few hours earlier, which had broken both his wheels. In his career, there was often a bit of rough with the smooth. But at last, he had what he wanted. Draped over his chair was a woollen yellow jersey, with the initials of Tour founder Henri Desgrange over the heart and a stitched-on fragment just above, bearing his Gitane-Leroux team name.

Twenty-four hours later, it was already on a rival's back as Simpson lost several minutes in a time-trial up the climb of Superbagnères. The significance of his achievement lasted far longer than his spell in cycling's sacred garment. Simpson had joined a select historical club and founded one of his own for Great Britain. The country's first yellow jersey was a symbol of its future potential. "Simpson did more than lead the Tour de France; he showed that the day may now be near when an Englishman will win the whole race", George Pearson wrote in a subsequent *Cycling* editorial. Of course, Simpson himself intended to be the man to fulfil that prophesy. He saw his day on the throne as a springboard to taking the entire Tour de France kingdom.

Professional cycling revolved around the Tour de France then, and the tough three-week event still remains the sport's calling card to common man and connoisseur alike, renowned as the most prestigious race where the best riders in the world compete. In the 1960s, it was smaller and considerably less international than the modern Goliath,

Chatting to a gendarme in Aix-les-Bains, stage 19, 1962 Tour de France

Losing the yellow jersey after a mediocre performance against the clock on the relentless climb to Superbagnères, 1962 Tour de France

yet was still the biggest thing to tear through most French villages for years. Its passage was an assault on the senses, a hybrid of a parade, an invading army and a sporting event. Vehicles, clad in bulbous dioramas advertising various products, drove the route hours before the riders as part of the publicity caravan, toting freebies to the public. Then, among the crackle of transistor radios, the thud of helicopters overhead, the crashing of sirens and the burble of musical team car horns, the toned Tour peloton passed in a mechanical symphony. There might even be the odd accordion playing too.

The nostalgic patina lent by footage from Tours of the Sixties casts it as a glamorous, winsome national event, contested by cheery "Giants of the Road". In the words of the infamous soigneur Willy Voet, cyclists are warriors on the bike, but good actors off it. The speed, distance and quality field made the race a gruelling test. While most young cyclists romanticise the idea of competing at the Tour de France before they do it, Tom Simpson had a realistic initial reaction to a debut in 1960. "The Tour frightened me … it was so big, incomparably bigger and greater than anything I had tried. Over 4,000 kilometres in 21 days and only one rest day. No, thank you very much", he recounted in *Cycling*.

Within a matter of weeks, his mind had been changed by a chat with his manager Daniel Dousset in which that recurrent theme, money, cropped up. He couldn't afford *not* to ride the Tour: a stage win, spell in the yellow jersey or top-ten finish were all guarantees of a summer of lucrative criterium appearances and a potential pay rise. Despite his earlier trepidation, Simpson immediately got stuck in. Racing as part of a British national team, he joined a breakaway on the first stage and finished highly, despite crashing on entry to the finish on Heysel stadium's cinder track in Brussels. Ninth in the afternoon's time-trial had him in the hunt for the yellow jersey.

The next day, as the race crossed into France, Simpson made it into a six-man breakaway on the way through Dunkirk and became the leader of the Tour de France on the road. A Tommy on the warpath through one of the key D-Day

La Rochelle *en fête*,
1966 Tour de France

landing locations made for some easy newspaper copy. Only the pursuit of race leader Gastone Nencini's Italian team and the pragmatic tactics of three French national team riders accompanying Simpson prevented him from taking the yellow jersey. Near the finish in Malo-les-Bains, they attacked one by one. If he wanted to win, Simpson would be required to chase, the other two could save energy by staying in his slipstream, then it would be their turn to repeat the move if the attacker was caught.

René Privat escaped for victory and Jean Graczyk came off Simpson's wheel to take second place, snatching the 30 bonus seconds on offer that would have put the Briton in the race lead. Simpson was left disappointed, but he was still the whirlwind of the race's first week. *L'Equipe* remarked: "At Lille, he had his little reputation. At Brussels, we started to consider and observe him curiously. At Saint Malo, he worries Anglade, Nencini and [Jan] Adriaensens. They fear him, they watch him, they afford him a thousand little attentions, the kind reserved for the lords of the bunch … Simpson has become one of the central figures of this Tour de France, to the point that he is annoyed. He's not used to such solicitude."

Negation followed sensation. For the rest of the week, Simpson's moves were regularly marked by rivals whose teams had greater numbers and strength in depth. In 1960, the race structure was uneven: France, Belgium, Italy and Spain had 14 riders each; Germany, Great Britain, The Netherlands, a mixed Swiss-Luxembourg side and the four French regional squads only had eight.

Simpson's inexperience contributed to seven crashes in the first ten stages. The sore first-timer continued to overshoot his limits when the race hit the mountains. These are where the Tour is

150

In pain and fighting
to stay in yellow,
1962 Tour de France

usually won and lost, where fortunes can be quickly reversed and faint time gaps can widen into chasms. He fell again on the descent of the Col d'Aubisque, winning the prize for the day's unluckiest rider, while his attempt to follow eventual winner Gastone Nencini's move over the Col de Peyresourde into Luchon, 24 hours later, backfired spectacularly. "I could do nothing – not even breathe or see straight. I have never been in such a state", he told *Sporting Cyclist* afterwards. In the Alps, he fell at the foot of the Col d'Izoard and several competitors rode over his calf, which left him limping to the finish in Paris. The rest of the British team were similarly beaten up. After Vic Sutton quit three days before the end, Robinson and Simpson were all that remained of the original octet.

The debutant finished the Tour 29th, but the summer criteriums were just beginning. "Now the hard work starts", Simpson said, as his manager handed him his packed schedule in the Parc des Princes stadium. It was straight off to Normandy to compete the following day. Completely frazzled, Simpson left never wanting to ride another Tour, yet he returned 12 months later for an abortive race. Suffering with a nagging knee injury, he quit on day four, eliminated alongside three other Britons, including his old junior rival, Pete Ryalls.

That winter, it was all change for Simpson, as he joined Raymond Louviot at Gitane-Leroux, a combination of old stars and hungry, young talent which fitted him well.

The Tour de France was evolving too. In a move that prefigured the contemporary format, directors Jacques Goddet and Felix Lévitan decided to run the 1962 edition with trade teams rather than national outfits. They were catching up with the sport's other top races: in the early Fifties,

151

1967 TOUR DE FRANCE: The peloton climbs
the Ballon d'Alsace on stage 8

1967 TOUR DE FRANCE: Barry Hoban stops to fill up his bidons during the thirteenth stage over Mont Ventoux to Carpentras

the rise of businesses financing squads in return for publicity took the strain off a cycling industry struggling to support teams in a period of soaring car and motorcycle sales. The Tour's head honchos feared commercial exploitation, but recognised the need to adapt; besides, the Tour was already a heavily materialistic venture. Fifteen teams of ten riders took to the 1962 Tour de France start line in Nancy, sponsored by the likes of coffee machine manufacturer Faema, household appliance vendor Philco and chicory makers Leroux.

On day one to Spa, Simpson was part of a 23-strong group that stole a march on the rest as feared climbers Federico Bahamontes and Charly Gaul were left minutes behind. The next day, Simpson's team was only beaten by Belgian squad Faema in a time-trial. The bunch swept west across northern France and towards the Pyrénées at a ferocious pace, as Rik Van Looy's Faema flunkeys set a red-hot speed, seeking stage wins for their leader/sprinter. There was no chance for a breather: this was a rare Tour without a rest day.

A first-year pro with Pelforth making his debut that year, Alan Ramsbottom recalls the experience as, "eye-opening. [It opened them to] the professionalism of a lot of the riders: the drugs. There were a lot around at that time. I went to the race with one suitcase. But the other riders had the same big one I had and another full of all kinds of medicaments, vitamins and tonics. Tommy Simpson had a doctor. He looked after that side for him."

The use of amphetamines and painkillers was widespread among the Tour's competitors. Amphetamines increase an individual's output by causing the rapid and complete consumption of energy reserves through nervous stimulation – they eliminate the sensations of fatigue, but not the fatigue itself. They took effect quickly and wore off that day, though there was the risk that they would rob a competitor of vital reserves later. And up to 1966, their use was technically legal.

The concept of anti-doping in sport is relatively modern: the first international framework

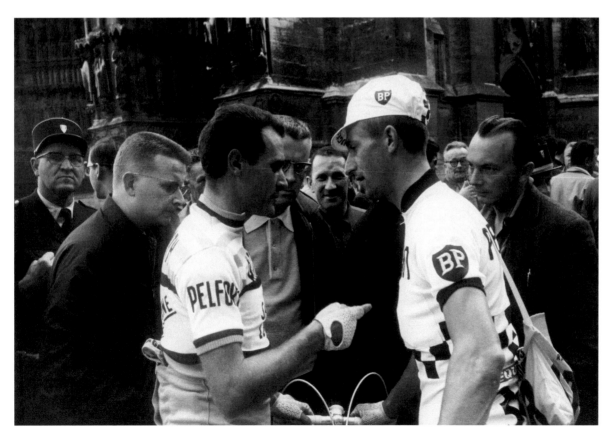

A few moments away from throwing a punch at Pelforth leader Henri Anglade, as they argue over the non-selection of his compatriot Alan Ramsbottom, 1964 Tour de France

was only drawn up by the Council of Europe in 1963 and French law banned and criminalised the use of stimulants in athletic competition two years later. Until then, there were no rules forbidding drug use, although several influential figures, including Tour doctor Pierre Dumas, expressed concern at some of the practices they witnessed in riders' bedrooms, such as IV drips and amphetamine injections. They were just another generation who used them to get through the race. In the past, anything and everything went: from the use of morphine and chloroform to doses of the poisonous alkaloid, strychnine. The 1962 Tour saw 14 riders leave the race at the ski station of Superbagnères. Their excuse was seafood, though it was probably dodgy morphine doled out by one soigneur. Something was certainly fishy. "Was it the *poisson* or the poison?" Raymond Poulidor quipped.

A day earlier, Simpson entered the first big Pyrénean stage of the race in third place overall. As race leader André Darrigade and Willy Schroeders were dropped over the Tourmalet,

Aspin and Peyresourde, Simpson took the yellow jersey by finishing with the favourites. His moment in the lead was short-lived: after his team manager Louviot advised him to put on higher gears than usual for the time-trial to Superbagnères, Simpson fell apart in the latter part of the climb and dropped to sixth overall. He was disappointed, not so much to lose the jersey, but to drop several minutes to the other contenders.

However, after a week of steady racing, he fought back to third place after the race's hardest stage in the Alps. Despite two punctures on the descent of the Col d'Izoard, at the end of a nine-hour day into Briançon, he rode intelligently to finish just over a minute adrift of favourites Poulidor, Imerio Massignan, Charly Gaul, Jef Planckaert and Jacques Anquetil. "I am not a great climber. If I try to keep with those fellows all the time on the mountain, I become asphyxiated. I prefer to drop back, pedal at my own rhythm and then rejoin in the descent", he told *The Daily Telegraph* afterwards.

Sunshine and light with Rudi Altig, 1966 Tour de France. Photograph by *Sporting Cyclist*

Simpson defends his sixth place overall against the clock, stage 20 between Bourgoin and Lyon, 1962 Tour de France

However, that tactic forced him to take greater risks. The next day, while chasing the leaders down the Col de Porte, Simpson miscalculated a gravel-strewn corner and went over the edge of the road into the adjacent forest. His bike flew into a tree and was fished down by a helpful French cameraman. Simpson rode over two cols to the finish, nursing a broken middle finger which was cast at hospital in Bourgoin that night.

It slowed him down for the decisive long time-trial around Lyon. Even in the best of nick, Simpson and company were powerless to compete with Jacques Anquetil in his outstanding discipline. Only Ercole Baldini finished within five minutes of the awe-inspiring "Monsieur Chrono". Finding it hard to hold the handlebars and, one report suggests, with a piece of paper stuck in his derailleur for the last 10 kilometres, Simpson lost 11 minutes to the Frenchman over the 62-kilometre course. However, he clung onto sixth place overall and won £100 as the "super unfortunate" of the race in Paris. Without his fall, Simpson reckoned he would have finished on the podium. It was his best Tour and a result not bettered by another Briton until Robert Millar finished fourth in the 1984 Tour de France.

Simpson rode a lap of honour at the Parc des Princes finish, struggling to simultaneously hold a giant bouquet of flowers, wipe away his tears and acknowledge the crowd's ovation with his one good hand. The *Daily Express* newspaper flew his mother Alice out to watch in the stadium. Speaking to the filmmaker Ray Pascoe, she remembered Simpson's coarse appearance: "His face: when he kissed you, you could feel the grit and the sand coming down on you … He used to say many times, 'you just put us in the way you'd put a racehorse, mother. We're fed, we're washed, we're looked after and [we] get on with the races.'"

The modern standard of care was decades away. After finishing a stage, riders usually pedalled 10 kilometres or so to find their lodgings, which were assigned by the Tour de France organisation. They ran the full gamut from châteaux to shitholes. 'The accommodation was abominable. A-bom-in-able", 1968 Tour de France winner Jan Janssen says, lengthening the syllables for emphasis. "We'd often be staying in school dormitories or brothels." Rest wasn't always straightforward either. During the 1964 edition, after finishing second to Jacques Anquetil on a stage to Monaco, Simpson took two cold showers and slept on the floor because of the heat. A year later in the Alpine town of Gap, the Peugeot team moved to a different hotel, unable to sleep as the Tour drivers and locals made a racket at a neighbouring film show.

"And the food, *oh la la*. The steak was like this", Janssen says, narrowing his index and middle finger to a wafer-thin wedge. "It was chicken, rice and spaghetti. Terrible." The supermarket SPAR provided food for riders during the race. At the stage start, riders filled their pockets with rice cakes, bananas, plums and sugar lumps; to drink, they had the choice of tea, coffee, lemon juice or peppermint mineral water. Each rider was handed a yellow musette at the mid-stage feed zone, usually containing ham or jam sandwiches, rice cakes, tarts and fruit. Competitors started the day with two water bottles and could have two more in their feed bag, but were forbidden from taking on more bidons directly from the team car by the race organisation. It's doubtful their managers would have been inclined to provide them anyway: guzzling too much water was seen as a weakness, the perception being that it would weigh down the stomach. In hindsight, it's clear that most riders of the era finished races badly dehydrated. The images of champions glugging post-stage bottles of Perrier take on a different dimension when you consider that they were parched.

During hot days, the Tour racers regularly slaked their thirst from fountains and taps in towns. Otherwise, there was the *chasse à la canette* – literally, the hunt for a can. A domestique would stop at a roadside bar and stuff whatever he could fit into his woollen jersey pockets from the fridge: wine, beer, cognac, Coca-Cola and even the occasional magnum of champagne. The conscientious team worker would carry a bottle opener and handkerchief with him to twist the bottle top off.

Every champion needed a fair few dedicated helpers on their team for far more than waitering. They were Sancho Panzas to the questing Quixote, at their disposition to close gaps, take the wind, chase down errant breakaways and numerous other tasks, however grim. During the 1967 Tour, Simpson commandeered the cotton casquette of his British team-mate Colin Lewis so that he could, according to the domestique, "take a shit".

Jacques Anquetil's most trusted disciples were Anatole Novak and Pierre Everaert, Raymond Poulidor relied upon Jean-Pierre Genet and Fausto Coppi had Ettore Milano. At the Peugeot team, where he raced from 1963 till his death, Simpson could rarely count on such dedicated support. "It was not like those tactics we see now, a team around their leader", his former team-mate Henri Duez recalls. "It was a lot more individualist. Sometimes, my team-mates—," he whistles and waves his hand, implying they'd be up the road in a flash. That's not to say there was a total absence of help: Duez recalls sharing a bidon of glucose with Simpson on a 1966 stage over the Aubisque and Tourmalet, leading to his own rapid loss of energy. But in the mid-Sixties, French team-mates like Désiré Letort, Raymond Mastrotto and Roger Pingeon often pursued their own agendas at the Tour.

Although Simpson was sometimes left under-supported, he couldn't claim to be a perennial victim of selfishness either. At the 1965 Midi Libre, faced with the then-unknown Pingeon leading the race into the final day, the race organisers made it clear that they'd prefer a more renowned winner. Chasing the prize money for winning, Simpson got into a breakaway and the bunch permitted its escape, only for him to puncture within sight of the finish line. Fellow escapee André Foucher won the race and Simpson finished third, in tears.

"We didn't seem to get organised like a lot of other squads. You usually have an understanding that if a break goes away and your team has a rider up there, you defend him", Alan Ramsbottom, who raced with Peugeot in 1965 and 1966, says. "But with us, it didn't go like that. A Peugeot

Simpson leads Rik
Van Looy and Rudi
Altig (in yellow), stage
2 from Charleville
to Tournai, 1966 Tour
de France

rider would get away and who brought him back? The Peugeot team."

Simpson's 1964 Tour de France bid was affected by perceived shoddy team backing. After an uncharacteristically conservative first week, Simpson was to the fore in the first decisive Alpine stage over the Télégraphe and Galibier into Briançon. However, two punctures on the final descent and a slow wheel change from the team car saw him lose a minute to the favourites. A week later, a long wait for his Peugeot management after another flat led to total meltdown.

This was the iconic stage where Jacques Anquetil lost minutes on the way over the Andorran climb of the Port d'Envalira, having over-indulged on roast lamb and red wine during the rest day. It was arguably Raymond Poulidor's best opportunity of his career to twist the knife and put the race out of his rival's reach.

But in thick fog, Poulidor and the leaders descended hesitantly while Anquetil, helped by the headlights of following press vehicles, pulled off a reckless drop to the valley and caught them. Near the top, he passed a stationary Tom Simpson,

159

waiting for mechanical assistance after another puncture. His Peugeot team-mate Raymond Mastrotto stopped and gave him a wheel. It was too little, too late: Simpson didn't catch up. "At Briançon, I lost one and a half minutes through my team car not being there. Today, I have lost two and a half more and any chance of getting near Anquetil. I'm fed up and have completely lost interest in the Tour", he told *The Daily Telegraph*. Simpson blamed team manager Gaston Plaud, and said that he was done with Peugeot. At this point, he was still tenth overall, within seven minutes of the favourites, but he fell back to finish a distant 14th.

Plaud defended himself from Simpson's accusations. However, questions have been raised by his former charges over his managerial prowess. Often inviting the local Peugeot rep to dinner at races, it seemed Plaud's public relation skills were more incisive than his tactics. "He was too nice to be a directeur sportif. If Gaston was stricter, we would have won a lot more races", Emile Daems says. "Sometimes, you need to bang your fist on the table to put things in place. He never shouted."

Supported by team-mate André Zimmermann on the stage from Montpellier to Mont Ventoux, 1965 Tour de France

"In the 1963 Paris-Brussels, Tom Simpson was there with Jean Stablinski, who was world champion. Simpson had a problem with his chain and Stablinski attacked and won. The rest of us went to Gaston Plaud afterwards, we weren't happy because we spent all day braking and slowing things down behind. Plaud said 'it doesn't matter, everyone did everything they could.' For him, it was normal. But I find that when we ride like that for 300 kilometres, to lose the race in the final kilometre is a catastrophe."

Andre Desvages's blunt assessment of Plaud is "completely incompetent". He alleges that the Peugeot riders rarely saw a franc of prize money from the team's successful 1967 Paris-Nice and Milan-Sanremo campaigns because Plaud sequestered it for himself. In a separate colourful anecdote, he recalls taking his team manager by the shirt collar and asking him for the money he was owed in no uncertain terms.

Simpson himself acknowledged Peugeot's shortcomings. "I could win the Tour de France one day, but not with the team I'm with", he told *The Sunday Times* in 1966. Regarding his team-mates' half-hearted support, he said: "It's only natural. They're French. I'm English. If we had an English team – and I could pick 10 very good men riding on the Continent right now – it would be a different story." Though it no doubt scanned well at home, this is a dubious claim: when the Tour briefly reverted back to national team format in 1967, Great Britain was one of the weakest units. They finished 13th out of 13 in the team time-trial and by the halfway point, five team members had abandoned, exhausted.

There were occasions when Simpson looked to leave for a different team. He had offers from Ignis and Romeo during his time there. In the summer of 1965, with Simpson's contract up for expiry, Plaud trapped him with a Catch-22 ultimatum: sign for the next two years, or you won't even be racing the Tour. In order to get a contract elsewhere, Simpson knew he'd have to perform in cycling's definitive shop window. Ultimately, it was a case of "je t'aime … moi non plus" with both Peugeot and the Tour.

"If I didn't have to ride it, I wouldn't. Because it's a so-and-so, it's a swine of a race", he says in *The World of Tommy Simpson*. Yet with the eye-watering money that could be made from success – Simpson reckoned that victory would earn a rider £30,000 the following year (around £636,000 today) – as well as the chance to leave an indelible mark in history, the Briton always entertained the prospect of victory.

The million-franc question is, how does one win the Tour? Two-time champion Antonin Magne described the process as "a spider's web that you spin practically every day, with method and perseverance. One lone slip and the whole thing tears." This technique was the preference of five-time winner Jacques Anquetil, who combined consistent climbing with knockout time-trials. In contrast, Simpson was a freedom fighter who liked to attack the conservatives around him. His efforts to win with outstanding panache were fool-hardy. Being a man of impulse, such an advantage in one-day Classics, might win the battle, but rarely the Tour war.

"You've got to be clever and to have the legs", Jan Janssen says. "For my Tour de France win in 1968, I had to carry off an exploit in the final day's time-trial or I wouldn't win. I was a rider who could take responsibility in the race. I said, 'I'm maybe not the best, but I am the smartest.'"

With only three team-mates left in the race to help him, Janssen mentally wore down the incumbent leader, Herman Van Springel. "The last few days, I said to him: 'Herman, you're not going well, eh? You're sluggish on the bike.' Things like that." Janssen had channelled his reserves better and leapfrogged his rival to win without ever racing in the *maillot jaune*.

"I knew riders who couldn't support the pressure of the race. It is a mental challenge. I was very strong in the mind, I had self-confidence, thinking 'who is going to beat me?' Simpson had a very strong mentality too, he was a fighter. At the start, the feed zone or 100 kilometres from the finish line, you always had to watch out for Tommy Simpson. Because he had good ideas. A lot of riders had respect for Simpson because

On the attack again, stage 1, 1965 Tour de France

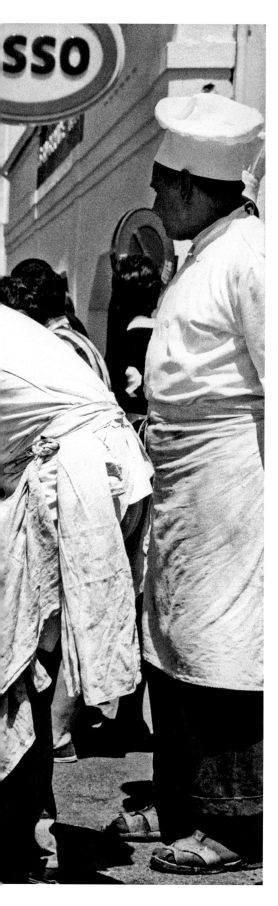

A chef roars Simpson on from the roadside, 1966 Tour de France

he liked to thrash himself ... he was no follower, not always glued to the wheel."

Could Simpson win the Tour de France? "My impression is that Tommy was too nervous. He was shrewd, but laissez-faire. Why attack at the start when we still have 200 kilometres to go? Above all when there's a little col just after the start. Tommy was nice and fun, but he was not always clever."

Sometimes, while looking to blow up the race, Simpson would end up exploding himself. "He gave so much, he was in a break and would do three-quarters of the work by himself", says Peugeot team-mate Henri Duez. "The first col was *à bloc*, everyone else lined out behind him. The second col was the same, and then the third, you know who would be at the back? Tom. He was cooked. He didn't know how to conserve his energy."

"In the Tour de France, sometimes he'd say to us: 'I'll take the jersey tomorrow,' like before the stage to Briançon [in 1966]. Then he cracked on the Galibier. He was proud of being English, he always believed that he would be the first Englishman to win the Tour. But only he thought that."

Simpson's compatriot Vin Denson agrees. "I said to him 'you could win it', but I never thought Tom was any good for more than about ten days. Paris-Nice or the Dauphiné suited him fine. He was good at stage races because he could recover well ... When it came to the Tour, he had too much aggression, he was too nervy, too spasmodic. He could keep cool and calm for a week. After that, you didn't know what he was thinking, whether he was going to attack and go in a break or not."

It's debatable whether stealing into breakaways before the race's high mountains was self-defeating panache or, in fact, Simpson's best shot at winning the race. He accepted his limitations in the high mountains, unable to regularly stay with Bahamontes, Poulidor and Jimenez, the period's best climbers. Gaining time in the Tour's flatter opening ten days, then defending a lead tooth-and-nail in the Alps and Pyrenees was a viable route to victory, borne out by contemporaries Roger Walkowiak, in 1956, and Lucien Aimar a decade later.

However, he had another weakness too. "After about ten days, you knew very well Tom was going to have an accident. If anyone was, it'd be him", Denson says. "He was prone to falling off or catching his leg on something." Some of this can be chalked down to bad luck, some is purely reckless bike handling. Falls affected his challenge in 1962, 1964 and 1966. In the latter edition, his Peugeot team crashed in the TTT and Simpson later hit a hay bale, the era's basic concession to health and safety, in a finish at Caen, losing 22 seconds.

The almost-literal tipping point came on stage 16 that year. Simpson attacked over the Col du Télégraphe and got to the giant Col du Galibier alone and in front. However, he blew up near the top, was passed by the favourites and was knocked off by a motorcyclist while chasing on the descent, hurting his elbow and thigh. He quit the race the next day with serious shoulder pain.

He regarded crashes as occupational hazards. "Oh, I have fear. Everyone does. I don't like going to the dentist", he told *The Sunday Times*. "I've been over the side several times but it doesn't *worry* me. I think it's the fact I get carried away with the race. There are times – if you stop to think about it – where I've fallen and I've thought 'gorblimey, just another inch or two and it'd be finished.'"

At times, Simpson felt as if the fates were against him at the Tour. He narrowly missed out on a stage win several times: on consecutive stages in the 1966 Tour, he finished second to Rudi Altig and Georges Vandenberghe. After his 1965 race was derailed by bronchitis and a bad infection, he wrote in his autobiography: "Most of all, I would like to win the Tour de France but I cannot afford to have any bad luck, such as in past attempts."

There was some sense to Simpson's fervent optimism too. Approaching his physical prime, he sensed that he could fill the power vacuum between Anquetil, the outgoing dictator, and the sport's next champion. History proves him right: between 1965 and the start of the Merckx monopoly in 1969, there was a succession of opportunistic Tour winners.

For all his bravado, Simpson had a blinding flash of candour in the autumn of 1965. "I've taken time to understand it, but it's done: I am not a Tour man", he told *L'Equipe* after winning the Tour of Lombardy. "Now, I will start the race relaxed to play the team helper role for Pingeon, for example." His timing is telling: he is talking as world champion, at the summit of his earning power and cycling status, when he least needed to entertain delusions of Tour grandeur. He resolved that he would not dream about cycling's biggest race anymore, that it didn't attract him as an aim. Yet, come next June that would seemingly be forgotten and Simpson was throwing his casquette into the ring again. In an era without specialisation, where a Tour contender was – and had to be – equally motivated for Paris-Roubaix, the Tour de France or the Tour of Lombardy, there was no backing away from a challenge.

Before the fateful 1967 race, Simpson's need for a Tour de France result had reached fever pitch. He was racing for his future financial security: he had a contract provisionally agreed for himself and Vin Denson at the Italian squad Salvarani for the next year, but needed proof of his ability to increase its value. "I have to show that I am a Tour man, prove that I can be a danger, and I have not done that yet", he told journalist Geoffrey Nicholson before the race start in Angers. Simpson believed he needed to hold the yellow jersey for several days, win a couple of stages or finish on the podium.

Winning the Tour de France became the thing Simpson wanted most of all, but it was probably the race that suited him the least. There were too many factors stacked against him: a lack of cohesion at Peugeot or strength-in-depth when racing with Great Britain, an unwillingness, or inability, to curb his enthusiasm towards pragmatism and his own deficiencies in the high mountains. This refusal to accept limitations or kowtow to the prescribed way of winning is part of the Simpson charm. But his ardent desire to prove his Tour de France threat to the world would play a big part in his undoing.

Tucking into a peach in Carpentras before stage 15, 1965 Tour de France

166

168

BREAKING BRITAIN

"I presume that Tom Simpson will become an illustrious figure in his home country this morning", Tour de France race director Jacques Goddet wrote in his *L'Equipe* column after Tom Simpson secured Britain's landmark first yellow jersey in 1962. "He deserves it too because this boy has a shining personality and the class of a very well-rounded cyclist."

Goddet was lord of all he surveyed in the anarchic mobile village of the Tour, an eloquent writer and Oxford-educated Anglophile. However, he was well wide of the mark in his estimation of Simpson's fame. "If it's raining at Wimbledon, I'll undoubtedly be lucky to have some articles a little bit longer than usual in the press", Simpson said. "Otherwise, it risks going unnoticed." He did make the front page: at the bottom of *The Daily Telegraph* opener on July 6, tucked away below news of a mediocre first day at the crease for England versus Pakistan, the preview of the first women's Wimbledon final between married women for 48 years, and a shooting in newly independent Algeria, a 50-word nib is entitled "Englishman leads". It goes on to erroneously state the nationality of his closest challenger, Ab Geldermans, as Belgian.

Wowing the Continental public was one thing, but breaking Britain was quite another. Simpson was only a hero to the small cycling fraternity back home. A Gallup International Poll from 1955 indicates the sport's humble standing: from 1000 people asked if they followed or participated in a sport, only five per cent responded with cycling. It languished in joint 17th place, alongside bowls, golf, dog racing and rugby league. Simpson's yellow jersey represented a starting point for increasing the sport's awareness. Five months later, he wore it on stage at the BBAR Concert at the Royal Albert Hall and received a standing ovation from the 5,000-strong crowd. He was the charismatic man to help develop the sport and its popularity back home.

Having spent his cycling adolescence during the warring years of the NCU and BLRC organisations, Simpson understood how far the

Smiling for the camera at the Herne Hill Good Friday Meeting, 1964. Photograph by Gerry Cranham

Tom and Bernard Burns lead the bunch, 1965 London to Holyhead. Photograph by John Otway

British racing scene lagged behind its Continental counterparts. Road racing on the open roads was only legalised in 1960 and cycling clubs still retained a whiff of a secret society. There were plenty of rites of passage, whether it be learning the ropes through gruelling weekend rides, deciphering outwardly unintelligible time-trial course codes, or figuring out which sprockets to use for certain scenarios. You didn't just become a club cyclist by paying a membership fee, you had to learn it and earn it. It was the pleasure of the hard-won.

The European racing milieu possessed an air of impenetrability, with news from abroad confined to weekly reports in *Cycling* or Jock Wadley's monthly *Sporting Cyclist*. For Britain's top roadmen, those 21 miles between Dover and the Continental mainland could feel like a quantum leap, such was the difference in culture, provision, quality, rhythm and distance of races, as well as the attitude to the sport. Unfamiliarity often bred inferiority. Given the lofty status of

modern British cycling, it's difficult for most to imagine how foreign this world was. In 1955, none of the riders in Britain's first Tour team, backed by the bicycle makers Hercules, could communicate in French. Some members of the party even put sugar in their wine because of the peculiar taste. It was the preserve of desperado adventurers: one hardy trio, John Andrews, Vic Sutton and Tony Hewson, drove over and lived in a bulky Austin ambulance in 1958, setting up camp in Reims. Aside from the pioneer Brian Robinson, the rest struggled to make ends meet in this cutthroat environment.

Into the Sixties, the newly formed British Cycling Federation regularly sent teams to the Peace Race and the Tour de l'Avenir, but going from these tough amateur events to the sport's biggest race was still like climbing five rungs on a ladder at once. Ahead of the 1961 Tour de France, the last edition of the permanent international team era, several of the dozen British team members had to get time off work,

172

Simpson to the fore with Keith Butler on his wheel and Barry Hoban furthest right, 1965 Corona Grand Prix

epitomising the professional-amateur divide: Albert Hitchen was a locomotive engineer, Ken Laidlaw a carpenter and Pete Ryalls served in the Army. They arrived at the start in Rouen with their own racing equipment, much of it inferior to their rivals. Luckily, the Italian parts manufacturer Campagnolo was staying in the same hotel and happily put their gear on numerous bikes.

When the race hit the mountains, team manager André Mater, a brothel owner in Paris when he wasn't directing cyclists, would routinely head over to the French national team's hotel to shoot the breeze. In the process, he'd find out what gears Jacques Anquetil and company were using for the long climbs and report back to the mechanics so that the Britons – down to a trio for the final fortnight – could copy them. On one hand, the Tour's subsequent reversion to trade teams snuffed out an opportunity for raw Britons to compete in and learn from cycling's big race; on the other, it ensured that their next crop of

talent earned selection for the Tour on merit, not by their passport.

Alan Ramsbottom and Vin Denson both headed to Troyes in north-central France, turning pro with Pelforth in 1962 and 1963, respectively, after shining in the amateur ranks. The following year, Barry Hoban signed with Mercier. "I started thinking if Tom can do it, I can do it", Hoban recalls. However, it was difficult for Englishmen to be assured of a place at the leading races. The sport's trade teams were still run along strong patriotic lines, with rider selection predicated on their sponsor's dominant market and initial rules which stipulated six riders per team had to be of the same nationality.

Then, there were problems behind the scenes. Alan Ramsbottom remembers his salary being withheld for several months. "They made it difficult for you. You've still got to buy food and eat; if you're not eating right, you're not riding right", he says. "It was because we were British. Vin Denson and I ended up having to drive all the way up to Dunkirk [from Troyes], about 300 miles, to get some money. Our manager Maurice De Muer kept saying 'you Brits are always short of money.' Because we weren't getting paid regularly."

When Denson joined Solo-Superia in 1964, he was only the second non-Belgian on board. There was a perception that he was taking bread from their compatriots' mouths. "An Englishman had to be streets better and work twice as hard to get a place", Denson says. Going through similar hardships brought the few Britons together and helped to engender a siege mentality. "Tom would do better thinking of Britain than his team, he never ever thought a great deal of Peugeot", Denson says. "He used to say to me regularly: 'I'd bloody die for Britain, as soon as I've got that Union flag on my shoulders.'" Simpson was the nucleus of the ex-pat British cycling universe: by 1965, Hoban, Denson and Ramsbottom had moved to Ghent to be part of his tight-knit Anglophone gang.

A spate of British amateur hopefuls followed the Simpson model, heading over to Brittany or Belgium to race, hankering for a similarly meteoric ascent. In Ghent, the Café Den Engel and its dormitories became a home away from home for young dreamers. While he knew deep down that few would make the cut, Simpson was willing to impart his wisdom to the wannabes. He made £16 per head on a two-week training camp with Classics champion Fred De Bruyne and Belgian team manager George Ronsse in the spring of 1962.

Keith Butler was one of the few Britons to make it through the competitive Belgian circuit, racing as a pro between 1964 and 1967. It was a struggle to make ends meet: he earned £35 a month in his first year, which left little to support his family after food and rent. There was another daunting difference to British racing, as Butler witnessed at one Dauphiné Libéré stage. "Just before the start, I remember going past the chemist's and everybody crowded in. I was standing there like a lemon. I didn't even know what to ask for. But there we are, innocence", he says.

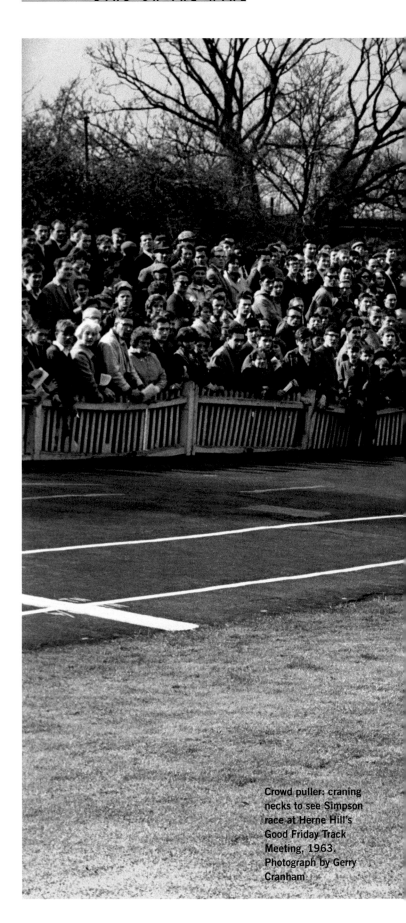

Crowd puller: craning necks to see Simpson race at Herne Hill's Good Friday Track Meeting, 1963. Photograph by Gerry Cranham

174

The essentially amateur nature of British racing insulated its competitors from that side of the sport. However, in the early Sixties, the racing calendar was expanding, having caught the eye of businesses outside the sport to support road races. Soft drinks brand Corona became patrons of the marathon London to Holyhead, the Tour of the South-West and their own eponymous grand prix. Meanwhile, the Manx Premier Race on the Isle of Man was enjoying a purple patch. Having attracted the likes of Fausto Coppi, Jacques Anquetil and Louison Bobet in the late Fifties, they now had a home hero to cheer. Simpson won in 1963 and 1967; his first victory came in such wet weather – typically for a British champion, Simpson felt that he raced better in such conditions – that Rik van Looy and Raymond Poulidor abandoned long before the finish. On the soaked winner's return to the

hotel after the race, the great Belgian champion led a round of applause for him.

This was one of Simpson's occasional home-comings. If the price was right, he would cross the Channel to compete during the season. "He and Hoban didn't have a lot of respect", says Dave Bonner, a Surrey-born national pursuit champion and top roadman of the Sixties. "They used to get invited when there was a race with good prize money and turn up with a load of Belgians. We were in there every week riding, then suddenly 100 quid first prize, there comes Tom. The whole lot used to all work for him or Michael Wright. We didn't stand a chance."

At the 1964 Corona Grand Prix at Crystal Palace, Simpson arrived with Peugeot team-mates Henri Duez and Georges Van Coningsloo, as well as fellow ex-pats Ramsbottom and Elliott. Simpson, Ramsbottom and Elliott quickly broke

Simpson is poised in fourth place as team-mate Camille Le Menn forces the pace, 1964 Manx Premier Road Race

away and unceremoniously lapped the bunch. Simpson, never one to rest on his laurels, then went to the front and split the group again. Sections of the crowd mocked them with a slow hand-clap and shouted "Bring back the school-boys", in reference to the more hotly contested 15-mile race fought out earlier that afternoon by the youngsters. In their own chasing group behind the breakaway, only Van Coningsloo and Billy Holmes resisted the humiliation. "I think we'd have been all right if we'd been racing all the time. I was a draughtsman and I trained at night: out the factory gates, I did 60 miles on my way home and got back at nine o'clock", Holmes says. At times, Simpson displayed an arrogance towards his amateur countrymen – he delivered the withering epithet "what a bunch of old men" after watching a Milk Race stage finish that summer – and a them-versus-us mentality

developed. It led to a fierce compulsion on the part of many top British racers to beat their sporting figurehead, rather than the deference Simpson might have hoped for.

Dave Bonner remembers a 1966 meeting at his local track, Herne Hill, with the world champion on the comeback trail from a broken leg. "There were three races [behind dernys] – five, ten and 15 miles", Bonner says. "Simpson said to me 'I've got to win it overall, but I'll win the first one, you win the second and I win the third.' I said to him 'no, we'll do that in the first two races but we'll *race* the last one.' And he wouldn't agree to it."

The first pair of races went to plan. In the third, Simpson suffered a mechanical. "I lapped the field two or three times before he got back in again. Then, they put him with me. Well, that wasn't right, why should they put him two or three laps up when he hadn't done it?"

At the Good Friday Track Meeting, Herne Hill, 1961. Photograph by Len Thorpe

1964 HERNE HILL:
Simpson waits to be
pushed off at the start
of the keirin

1964 HERNE HILL: Getting off to a flyer at the Good Friday Track Meeting. Photographs by Gerry Cranham

1967 LA CIPALE: Four stars of the
Sixties at a track meeting in
Paris: Simpson, Jacques Anquetil, Rudi Altig
and Eddy Merckx

1964 HERNE HILL: Resting between races with English time trialling ace Alf Engers (left). Photograph by Gerry Cranham

Up before dawn
for the start of the
275-mile one-day
marathon, 1965
London to Holyhead

"When we crossed the line, I put my hands up as the winner. And then they announced Simpson winning. I went round to protest, my manager stopped me before I got there and said to me: 'they've doubled your money.' Simpson got booed, the crowd knew I'd won."

At the other extreme from the track meets and city-circuit races which populated the British scene was the marathon London to Holyhead. It was billed as the longest non-paced one-day race in the world, a 444-kilometre trek from the capital to Newry Beach on the Welsh island of Anglesey. Eat your heart out, Bordeaux-Paris: the very race for which Simpson was preparing when he lined up for the start at Marble Arch in May 1965. Setting off in five o'clock darkness, the 37-strong bunch shot off into Hertfordshire and onto the A5 for a rolling ride. The roads were not closed; the competitors squeezed past buses and stopped at the infrequent red lights – just as well too, considering a policeman was hiding in Dunstable, waiting to apprehend any lawbreakers. Belgian rider René Van Meenen, visiting from the Continent alongside Hoban, Denson and

182

Elliott, probably didn't know what to make of it all. Part of an eight-man lead group in the race's finale, Simpson wanted to ensure a win with help from his cosmopolitan combine. It would please fans and the press, and his fellow Continentals' assistance would be generously rewarded. "Tom said 'I'll pay such and such to take the win off you'", Vin Denson recalls. "Shay and I were quite hard up, we needed some money, so we decided to ride for him."

"Barry [Hoban] attacked us before the finish, I jumped over and sat on his wheel, then the others came round. Then they had a bit of a worry with [Albert] Hitchen, I remember Shay Elliott had to hold him off", Denson says.

Simpson won all right, but the photograph of the sprint finish elicited controversy in the British press because runner-up Shay Elliott's fingers were visibly over his brake levers. It appeared he was blatantly making sure he wouldn't accidentally pip the arranged victor on the line. Simpson had sold the race: it wasn't honest, but a common part of the game then, as it is now. As the Briton once said, "A professional cyclist does not ride for fun, he rides to earn money." Besides, there was no deception with the pace: covering the route in a shade under 11 hours, it was the fastest ever edition of London to Holyhead.

Within a couple of months, Simpson had entered the heyday of his career, with a dream autumn of World Championship and Tour of Lombardy glory. His victory in San Sebastian, an underdog triumph achieved with a smaller, inferior team to his rivals, was proof that a British team could beat the Continentals at their own game and Simpson's entry into the mainstream. The man on the street could get his head round a world title, even if the likes of Milan-Sanremo and Ronde van Vlaanderen titles had led to head-scratching. In the winter of 1965, Simpson won a trio of top awards, most notably the BBC Sports Personality of the Year. Underlining his standing, he beat Jim Clark, who had won his second Formula 1 title, and the showjumper Marion Coakes into second and third places.

Simpson was a rare and perverse thing, a very British sporting champion who owed his success to spending his adult career away from its shores. But his worldly ways chimed back home in a mid-Sixties modern culture which appreciated style. He was a picture of Continental elegance with an English edge, who wore Lacoste and Fred Perry shirts on rest days. This effortless fashion must have gone down particularly well with the Mods. There was not much reciprocation: Simpson didn't particularly care for music, asking his wife Helen to pick his records for Desert Island Discs, and expressed his dislike for the beatnik culture to French journalist Michel Thierry: "England is an old country that needs a shake-up."

His year in the rainbow jersey coincided with a time of great prosperity and cultural upheaval back home. London was swinging and a string of fresh British national treasures, many of which are still beloved, were establishing themselves in the nation's consciousness too: James Bond, Coronation Street, Doctor Who, Bobby Moore and the World Cup winning team, David Hockney and Peter Blake, the Kinks, the Rolling Stones and, of course, the Beatles. British cycling's own beat-all experienced his own "Simpsonmania", even if it wasn't quite packed stadiums of screaming fans. He was mobbed by autograph hunters who spilled onto the track at Herne Hill. At another meeting on the Salford Park track, *Cycling* reports that Simpson "turned out in Solihull CC colours, finding his racing vest had been spirited away by a souvenir hunter."

At the height of his popularity, Simpson was still at ease juggling the micro and the macro. In December 1965, he found time to visit his old primary school, North Border Junior School in Bircotes, to give tips and present cycling proficiency certificates to pupils. Simpson wanted to use his profile and influence to boost the entire domestic sport too. After receiving the Sportsman of the Year trophy from prime minister Harold Wilson at the annual dinner of the Sports Writers' Association a fortnight later, he said: "You can be sure that, so far as I am concerned, when once I have ceased riding as a pro, you will be able to depend on me to do anything for cycling in Britain … I hope that industry will one day wake up to the possibilities of cycling. My dream is that one day we will have an English team sponsored by an English concern."

It was ambitious, yet there was a precedent. The bicycle manufacturer Hercules had backed a British team's debut in the 1955 Tour de France. The theory was that some English industry players could act as sponsors through the French subsidiaries they used to sell goods on the Continent. Simpson followed through his words with actions too. He had meetings with big business and was left disappointed when mid-1967 discussions in London with cycling industry top brass led nowhere. "They haven't understood that a professional racing cyclist can keep his word", he told journalist René de Latour. "They already let me know indirectly that they were going to take elsewhere the small fortune that they would have distributed building a team around me as a leader … It's a shame. I like money a lot. Not for me, but for Helen, Jane and Joanne."

Originating from a traditional cycling country might have automatically made his life – and meetings with the bank manager – a little easier. When asked whether he would take Belgian nationality in 1967, Simpson replied: "No, I'm proud of being British. But if I was a Frenchman, I'd get paid more, as much as Poulidor. And I would be the number two Frenchman, not Poulidor – I'd be the one to beat Anquetil."

He did pretend to be "a Froggy" on one winter return to Britain in 1960. At a closed level crossing gate in Newark, the impatient Simpson roared to the front of the queue on the right side of the road. When confronted, he pretended to be a foolish Frenchman and got away with it. This quick-wittedness was a mark of origin too. "English he was, English he always will be because he has this delicate touch of humour that his adversaries – whatever class or country – so miserably lack", wrote the journalist Jean Bobet.

Simpson's racing returns to home soil, given their infrequent nature, were big opportunities for publicity. A week before the start of the 1967 Tour de France, Corona publicity man David Saunders wanted to showcase the British team at some profile-boosting races on home turf. Big business got on board: there was a criterium at the Lancashire seaside town of New Brighton, sponsored by Player's cigarettes, and the Vaux GP in Country Durham, supported by the eponymous brewer. Simpson had privately expressed his displeasure at the lack of cycling coverage in the British media; here was a gilt-edged opportunity.

Yet, his last weekend in the UK was a comedy of errors. A mix-up with delayed aircraft and baggage at Heathrow Airport on the way to Manchester made Simpson and the band of accompanying Continental pros, Barry Hoban, Michael Wright and Alain Le Grevès late – so late that they missed the race. But with 12,000 fans packed on the promenade, alongside World of Sport TV cameras and the press pack, an ersatz one was hastily arranged. Ever professional, the latecomers borrowed bikes from members of the public and fellow riders; Simpson ended up winning on a young man's Tommy Soens. Some spectators went home especially satisfied: a young Brian Cookson, later to become president of the UCI, got his copy of *Cycling is my Life* signed by Simpson.

Simpson never made his anticipated racing appearance in the county where he was born. After the race, he explained to Corona publicity man David Saunders that he had been contracted to ride a coinciding track event in Vincennes the next day. An argument ensued, but his French engagement had to take precedence, for fear of expulsion from the Peugeot team, and he flew back to Paris that evening. Four weeks later, Tom Simpson was dead. The sport was robbed not just of a great champion and ebullient character, but a go-getting ambassador. In Simpson's absence, the hoped-for British invasion on two wheels did not happen: Barry Hoban was Britain's lone wolf in Europe in the Seventies. The dream of

184

Neck-and-neck with former Olympic team-mate John Geddes at the Manchester Wheelers' annual grand prix. Simpson's absence from the Tour de France, on the back of his Bordeaux-Paris victory, freed him up to compete at this popular July track meet, 1963

a conquering British-backed team also took decades to be fulfilled. ANC-Halfords spent several years racing on the Continent in the late Eighties, culminating in an eventful 1987 Tour de France appearance. But it wasn't until the success of British Cycling's grassroots-to-Olympics talent system and the arrival of Team Sky in 2010, that the inferiority complex was washed away. One wonders what Simpson would have done for British cycling governance and its development of top road racers. "He would have still been in cycling, believe me", Vin Denson says. "He said

that we wouldn't go back to England and do a nine to five job. We'll get an academy sorted, so the younger generation has something to go through on their way to France and Belgium. We'd say, what's the point of sending people up the hills with a load of sheep bleating at them?"

"But now, look at the difference. Tom would never have believed you'd have bike races down Buckingham Palace, past the Cenotaph, to have the Tour de France in London and millions of people coming out in Yorkshire, shouting bike riders on."

185

186

Chapter Nine

13 JULY 1967

On the start line at the
Tour de France, 1967

"There is special providence in the fall of a sparrow"

William Shakespeare

Just as the bicycle is a vehicle for forward motion, the professional cyclist's career is a perpetual process of rolling ambition. One finish line crossed and one disappointment digested, the next day is pregnant with possibility. Or the next race, the next month, the next season. On, on, on.

Unsurprisingly, in this hamster wheel of hope, Tom Simpson was not raging against the dying of the light in his final months. Asked if he thought he was at the peak of his career in a *Cycling* interview in April 1967, he replied: "By no means. What is a peak? When you reach a peak, you start going down. I just don't believe that." The long-term future was on his mind: he also spoke of his desire to leave the road scene during 1971 and mix family summer holidays with the winter Six Day circuit. To do that, he reckoned the need to squirrel away £50,000. However, Simpson's last big win was the 1965 Tour of Lombardy and he'd endured years of Tour de France mediocrity. His earnings were in danger of following his significant decline in results. Despite victory at Paris-Nice months earlier, Simpson needed a big performance to raise his salary at Salvarani. He built the 1967 Tour de France up into a make-or-break race.

"Last year I nearly went through without an off day, but then I fell and that was that. I've got no more excuses. At my age, I can't say I'll do it better next year. The only person I'd be kidding is myself", he told British journalist Geoffrey Nicholson. Simpson navigated that Tour's first

Conducting the orchestra: half of the Peugeot team ahead of the 1966 Tour de France (left to right) Ferdinand Bracke, Simpson, André Zimmermann, Georges Van Coningsloo, and (seated) Henri Duez

week without major problems, even joining a small breakaway over the cobblestones to Roubaix to steal a little march on a few rivals. With the race structure reverting to international teams, Simpson could rely on loyal British support, but limited strength-in-depth. Great Britain finished last of the 13 teams in the TTT, though 48 hours later, their Belgian-based sprinter Michael Wright won a stage, the nation's third in history.

Simpson planned to make his gains on three tough mountain stages where his rivals would be left exposed: stage 10 to Briançon over the highpoint of the race, the Col du Galibier, stage 13 to Carpentras over Mont Ventoux and stage 20's Puy-de-Dôme finale. But on his first D-day, Simpson was forced onto the defensive, fighting serious stomach problems over three Alpine climbs. He had to stop at the foot of the Galibier to empty his bowels and never regained contact

with the leaders. Taking risks on the twisting descent into the Alpine garrison city, he finished six minutes down on Felice Gimondi and Julio Jimenez, and just under three behind race leader Roger Pingeon and Franco Balmamion – distanced, but not yet defeated.

The ride brought home Simpson's extraordinary toughness, albeit for less attractive reasons. His bike, spattered in faeces, had to be washed down by a mechanic afterwards. Simpson was under the weather that evening too. "He couldn't hold down soup at dinner and was rushing to the toilet", his team-mate Vin Denson recalls. "He came out and wanted to go to bed. I took him upstairs … he was terrible, I was basically carrying him. Then the next morning, he was as bright as a button. He said he was hungry, he ate really well. We thought the fever had reached its peak, that he was okay now."

Sharing a joke with his Great Britain team-mates at the 1967 Tour de France (left to right): Vin Denson, Colin Lewis, Simpson, Arthur Metcalfe and Bill Lawrie

48 hours later, Simpson even sprinted to seventh place into Marseille on the eve of the Ventoux stage. It was another dehydrating day through great humidity in the French *Midi*. Putting a stiff upper lip on his suffering disguised the fact that he was still running close to empty. His Alpine episode of diarrhoea and vomiting pointed towards an infection. With such an alarming evacuation of food and fluids, he had a significant calorie deficit: 80 per cent of our fluid intake actually comes from food. On top of that, excessive consumption of water during stages was stigmatised and riders were limited to officially taking four bottles a day. Simpson's body was like a well that had run dangerously dry.

That night, Simpson dined with his agent, Daniel Dousset. The cash-conscious middleman reiterated the need to finish the Tour highly to ensure a better retainer from Salvarani the next year and his usual level of appearance money at the post-Tour criteriums. It left Simpson under even more pressure. He was seventh overall, just over eight minutes down on Roger Pingeon. Mont Ventoux needed to be the saviour of his Tour.

Simpson already had reason to fear the 1,912-metre climb. On his first time racing up it, at the 1960 Tour du Sud-Est, his freewheel block unscrewed near the top, necessitating a fierce chase down the other side to limit his losses. Then, there were his experiences on a stage finish there in the 1965 Tour de France. Writing in *Cycling*, Simpson described it as the only time he was scared in that year's race: "Suddenly, I ran into a real bad patch, everything went black before my eyes, like a veil, and quick as a flash I had no strength at all. This was about six miles from the summit, I think, I don't recall it very clearly.

I thought the skies were coming in on me and I just pedalled along in a daze without knowing what I was doing."

Helped by Salvarani team manager, Luciano Pezzi, who was passing him to drive behind his rival Felice Gimondi up the road, Simpson came through this mini collapse. After the finish, he had to wring out his shorts and socks, such was the volume of sweat in them. His result was not as bad as his sensations – he maintained his ninth place overall that evening – but it would have been natural to dread Mont Ventoux after that experience.

Ventoux is not the highest mountain on the Tour de France, nor is it the longest, steepest or the most difficult. But the ascent carries the most fearsome aura, one developed long before men on pushbikes arrived on its slopes. It is the geographical western terminus of the Alps, yet stands like an incongruous Gulliver among the surrounding Lilliputian lowlands of Provence, the summit visible for hundreds of kilometres around. Ever since Petrarch's Augustine spiritual awakening there in the 14th century, it has been ripe for allegory, providing a strenuous test of human moral, emotional and spiritual fibre.

The classic cycle racing ascent of Ventoux tackles its most difficult side, the 21-kilometre south-eastern climb from the town of Bédoin. Few other climbs in Tour lore possess such drastic and defined shifts in scenery. It has three distinct sections. There is the gentle rise up to the hamlet of Saint-Estève, past clicking cicadas and bucolic vineyards. Then, the road swooshes round a sole hairpin, straightens and pitches into a steep, unrelenting gradient through the deep forest of pine and beech trees. Last, and certainly not least, there are the famous, final six kilometres from the restaurant of Chalet Reynard, last vestige of civilisation, to the summit. The tree cover suddenly ends, replaced by an expanse of limestone scree. The air feels thinner and the heat seems to intensify, bouncing off those white *lauzes*. Most mountains, whether rocky and grandiose or charmingly verdant, are inanimate; Ventoux resembles a malevolent beast with

bipolar disorder. Given the microclimate at its summit, on any day, a cyclist might encounter 100mph winds gusting down the road, penetrate a dense cloud of mist or endure fuggy, furnace-like heat. That final segment, often likened to a lunar-scape by modern commentators, is the work of a nightmare weaver. The snow poles, black and yellow like hazard tape, which dot the open stretch to the summit scream warning; the red-white telecommunications mast on top goes teasingly in and out of visibility during the final kilometres, preying on a hypoglycaemic mind. Near the top, beauty and tyranny are side-by-side: look left and there is a vast panorama down over lavender fields and the Vaucluse plain; look right and the limestone banks tower. Little wonder the philosopher Roland Barthes called it "a damned terrain, a testing place for heroes, something like a higher hell."

Tom Simpson's story is intertwined with Mont Ventoux's modern legend, but the climb passed into notoriety for pushing Tour de France competitors beyond their physical limits before his arrival in France. Four years after its debut in the Tour, Jean Malléjac nearly died there in the 1955 race. The Frenchman zigzagged across the road before collapsing with one foot fastened to his toe clips, the other chillingly pawing the air with phantom pedal revolutions. He was unconscious for over 15 minutes, requiring an oxygen mask and an injection of the stimulant, solucamphor, from the Tour's doctor, Pierre Dumas. In the ambulance, Malléjac was in a state of confusion, shouting and demanding his bike to finish the stage. He later denied having taken performance-enhancing drugs. That same day, Louis Bergaud and Belgian rider Richard Van Genechten passed out too. It kickstarted Dumas's lobbying for concerted anti-doping legislation.

Joining the race as a doctor in 1952, Dumas's Tours of duty confirmed the prevalence of drugs in the sport during the Fifties and Sixties. He encountered riders on primitive IV drips and rattling pillboxes at night; by day, he occasionally even saw riders injecting themselves during the races. Amphetamines were the popular weapon of choice of the Sixties peloton. They flooded the market after a glut was produced during World War Two; according to one source, 72 million tablets were issued to the British forces. Allied and German pilots used Methedrine and Benzedrine to increase their alertness and confidence. Originally created as a decongestant, "bennies" filtered down into a high-speed, energetic society before their dangers were identified at the turn of the Sixties. They provided a boost for students pulling all-nighters and truckers on long-distance drives; the poet WH Auden popped the pills for 20 years to increase his work rate, Anthony Eden took them during the Suez Crisis and the actress Joan Sims was addicted to them.

These psychoactive drugs were popular as they took effect and wore off the same day. They were the popular stimulant of the era in a culture of cheating that had existed since the sport's first races. In the early 20th century, the pick-me-ups were even more eyebrow-raising: the likes of arsenic, nitroglycerine and coca sustained competitors, who endured exhausting stages in excess of 400 kilometres on bad roads. Given the full-on schedule, exhaustive drive to make money and the absence of any testing until 1966, it's hardly a surprise that drug use was commonplace for sportsmen inured to harnessing every possible gain. "You have to be an imbecile or a hypocrite to imagine that a professional cyclist who races 235 days a year in all weathers can keep going without stimulants", Jacques Anquetil once infamously stated.

In June 1965, a French anti-doping law was introduced, banning the use of stimulants in athletic competition, by pain of a prison term of a month to a year and a sizeable fine of up to £350. This was the first preventative measure

Messing about on boats in Marseille with Barry Hoban and Désiré Letort, stage 13, 1967 Tour de France

taken. Urine tests to detect amphetamine use followed at the Tour a year later. But they were ineffectual, the rules were enforced inconsistently and the riders still flaunted them, sometimes openly. When Jacques Anquetil said "Yes, I have taken stimulants today", after winning the 1966 Grand Prix des Nations time-trial, he was fined 2,000 francs but did not receive disqualification. He is still listed as the winner.

Noting the champions of the time who had a doping infraction would be a paragraph-long who's who of Sixties cycling: Merckx, Gimondi, Anquetil, Altig, Pingeon, Aimar and Rivière. Tom Simpson used banned stimulants too: had he not, it would have been remarkable. The peer pressure was persuasive too: you're either one of the gang or risk being marginalised – socially and financially – for refusing.

André Desvages, a pro with Peugeot between 1967 and 1970, unflinchingly puts the percentage of riders using doping products in that era as "a hundred per cent" – himself included. He remembers one 1965 Peace Race time-trial when, aware that there were no controls, he was administered a cocktail of anabolic steroids by a doctor and finished third. "It gives you more strength. You truly feel that you pedal faster than the others", Desvages says. Several other interviewees confirm that Simpson was well known for using stimulants. Vin Denson suggests that the doctor in their Gentse Velosport club, Vandenweghe, advised it. "Tom said to me, 'if you're riding 300 kilometres, that's not normal. Your normal would be 250 kilometres, then you're finished. Just the last 50, take eight milligrams of amphetamine and you'll be fine. You'll do more harm riding on nothing.'"

A top Sixties rider tells me 16 milligrams was the regular amount to take with another popular amphetamine, pervitin. As Paracelsus, the 16th century philosopher and physician wrote, the dose makes the poison. Over time, depending on a user's natural immunity and constitution, the amount needs to be increased to have a similar effect. In his autobiography, 1967 Tour de France winner Roger Pingeon claimed that Simpson

Great Britain rode a poor team time trial, finishing last and over five minutes adrift of stage winners Belgium, 1967 Tour de France

194

As usual, Simpson wastes no time going up the road, stage 1 between Angers and Saint-Malo, 1967 Tour de France

could take up to 100mg of amphetamines in one day, while a tenth of that was sufficient for him.

Sometimes, Simpson had recourse to more dangerous substances, such as the poison strychnine. "It is also a tonic, given in certain doses", Alan Ramsbottom says. "Tommy got some off his doctor, he was building up for a big race and had to take a little vial of this tonic every day. He did it for a full week during training. He took risks at times, did Tommy." The Briton recalls Belgium as a hotbed of pharmaceutical excess, remembering witnessing riders with hypodermic needles in their jersey pockets.

"Oh, the Belgians in the kermesses. They opened a box of Maxiton from their pocket, and they would put some on their tongue", Jan Janssen says. "Back then, [stimulants] Tonedron and Stenamina were very popular too." Tonedron was one of Simpson's favoured amphetamines, superior

to the more prevalent Benzedrine. According to his British team-mate Colin Lewis, Simpson paid £800 in 1967 for his year's supply, a sum that dwarfed most foot soldiers' annual salaries.

The riders often put their faith in soigneurs, the "carers" who massaged their charges after the race, prepared their feed bags and advised on or even administered pharmaceuticals. It was a shady, mysterious profession, with no qualifications, and was often difficult to discern beneficial wisdom from quackery. For instance, Simpson's trusted soigneur at Peugeot, Gust Naessens, liked to put boiled-up cattle feed into his man's water bottles. The sport had a pernicious lemming culture: old wives' tales, however bizarre or dangerous, were regularly accepted by subsequent generations chasing a cutting edge.

More could have been done by Tour de France race organisers Jacques Goddet and his predecessor

196

Henri Desgrange. Their roles as organisers and reporters were conflicting: they were ringleaders cracking the whip in the circus of pain then sending it up in the next day's newspaper. They prized the cult of suffering and the idea of the ultra-efficient man.

There had been plenty of chilling warning signs, with mere cosmetic measures, if any, taken rather than effective prevention. The sport and its competitors were playing a game of chance with their health, and Simpson was the unlucky man on the wrong day on the wrong mountain.

13 July 1967. As dawn broke on Marseille's historic central avenue, the Canebière, before the race's 13th stage, French journalist Pierre Chany bumped into Pierre Dumas outside his hotel. "The heat will be terrible today. If the riders dope, we will have a death on our hands", Dumas told him. A 211.5-kilometre stage awaited the bunch, heading north over the gentle rises of the Var and Luberon national park before going east in a loop over Ventoux and down to Carpentras. If Simpson was feeling the pressure ahead of this pivotal stage, he didn't show it on the start line. That morning at the Quai du Port in Marseille, he, Barry Hoban and Peugeot trade team-mate Désiré Letort messed around on a boat in the harbour for photographers. In the BBC documentary *Death on the Mountain*, the journalist Jean Bobet remembered a different Simpson, gaunt and white, who fixed him with a grimace and stuck his tongue out, on which he counted five tablets of Tonedron.

The stage started under a bad cloud when a dog ran into the peloton and caused an early crash, leaving Italian rider Marcello Mugnaini with a double arm fracture and Germany's Wilfried Peffgen with a broken collarbone. Otherwise, the early hours saw a gentle pace. The bunch slaked their thirst in the 40-degree heat at intermittent fountains and bars. During one bar run, Colin Lewis grabbed whatever he could for Simpson.

A few minutes down the road, when he had time to assess what he had purloined, he saw it was Coca-Cola and cognac. Simpson glugged his favourite soft drink first then requested the bottle of alcohol, saying "my guts are a bit queer". He took a few gulps and chucked it away.

Later in the day, Simpson ran into a bar at the foot of the Ventoux and had some more cognac. It was unusual for a leader to be drinking spirits on such a hot day and stopping at such a crucial juncture but with the mountain staring at him from the horizon for half the day, perhaps he felt the need for some French courage. His mechanic Harry Hall saw Simpson put some into his bidon and continue the race. The alcohol in his body was another losing roll of the dice. As a relaxant and depressant, it causes drowsiness, countering the stimulants he had put into an already overworked system on a scorching day.

As Poulidor came roaring past on the attack, helped by his domestiques, Vin Denson gave Simpson a helping hand. "I gave him a bottle of water, just as this group goes past. I think I led him out onto this back wheel of the group, he got Jimenez's wheel and off they went. It was such a hot day, getting on to the hundreds on Ventoux." For decades, Denson felt guilty about his subsequent final words to Simpson – *dai, dai*, Italian words for encouragement which sound like an incitement to keel over in English.

As Poulidor and Julio Jimenez escaped together, Simpson settled into a chasing group with other favourites Roger Pingeon, Felice Gimondi and Jan Janssen, determined to make good on his ambition to move up the ranks. One spot behind him in the Tour general classification, Janssen noticed Simpson's discomfort. "Everyone was suffering. Then I saw Tommy and he was white, as white as paper", he says, feeling the magazine page in front of him. "I made one more acceleration. And he was dropped. But I didn't know that it was so serious."

Great Britain manager Alec Taylor was driving the team car behind Simpson, accompanied by mechanics Ken Ryall and Harry Hall. They watched their leader drift backwards through another group, containing Lucien Aimar. Simpson's head began to crook to the right in a pronounced fashion, his telltale physical sign of suffering. As he climbed higher, the long-term effects of his diarrhoea and vomiting episode came further into play, affecting his body's ability to dissipate heat. "We control our temperature primarily through evaporative sweat loss – not sweat", says leading sports scientist and former Olympic modern pentathlete Professor Greg Whyte. "In a chronically dehydrated state, the whole body water content available to Simpson was greatly diminished. His ability to sustain sweat loss was lowered too: in layman's terms, he wouldn't be as good at sweating."

He was riding into a state of heat stress. Most normal people experiencing Simpson's symptoms would have stopped racing. But nothing about this pursuit was normal: the extreme nature of the Tour de France, his staunch ambition, the stifling heat, the demands of the milieu and the drugs in his system. "What you now have to factor in is that Tommy Simpson is taking amphetamines and methamphetamines which are a potent central nervous system stimulant", Whyte explains. "They are driving him to continue exercising. A movement from this heat stress into heatstroke ensues."

Two kilometres from the top of Mont Ventoux, Simpson started to zig-zag, experiencing dizziness and shortness of breath. His cardiovascular system was giving up. Simpson veered dangerously towards the left-hand side of the road, which had a drop onto rock below. As Hall prepared to leap out of the following car and stop him, Simpson corrected himself, only to go a few more yards and veer towards the shale bank on the other side. This was briefly captured by a following cameraman. The grainy footage shows Simpson's head sagging and his hands moving from hoods to drops before nearly falling over. You watch it in the hope that the next moments of recorded reality will somehow be different. This remains unprecedented in the history of the Tour de France, a man driving himself to death, and all caught on film. Coming at the end of a period when TV set sales soared, Simpson's death also became a notorious televisual event of the Sixties.

Harry Hall guided him to the bank at the side of the road. In a 1987 interview with *Cycling Weekly*,

Peugeot team-mate Désiré Letort and Simpson on the way to Mont Ventoux, stage 13, 1967 Tour de France

A crowd gathers as Doctor Dumas fights to save Simpson's life

he describes Simpson's last moments of lucidity: "I said 'that's it for you, Tom.' And I undid his [toe] straps. And at this point, he burst into 'no, no,' he wouldn't have that. 'No, no, get me up, get me up, get me up,' because he was in this awkward position of leaning against the bank … he was quite coherent. 'I want to go on, come on, on, get me up, get me straight.'"

"Me straps, Harry, me straps", he said, an instruction to tighten his feet in the pedals. These were probably Simpson's last words. The famous "put me back on my bike" line was likely a case of reported speech from Hall to *The Sun* reporter Sid Saltmarsh, who later asked if Simpson had said anything before he died. It virtually doesn't matter that he never uttered those words; the point is that his personality was so colourful and his determination so staunch, that he might have done. The line is full of pathos, but the meaning carries a dangerous myth. We often glorify the sacrifice of champions too readily, when Simpson shows that it can also lead to self-destruction.

On he went for another 400 metres until the same trouble struck. Riding to a standstill again and about to tumble into the road, Hall and Ken Ryall caught and guided him to the side of the road. Simpson was no longer conscious, but still poised ready to race, his back arched and hands wrapped around the bars. Ryall had to peel his fingers off them, so violently had his muscles cramped, due to a forceful spasm from his failing heart. Ominously, within a couple of minutes, Simpson had gone from sweat-slicked to dry and yellow-skinned. His body was in circulatory collapse, the classic end-product of heatstroke. As a crowd of spectators gathered around, Simpson's body was laid onto the milk-white scree and Hall started mouth-to-mouth resuscitation. Within a couple of minutes, the Tour doctor Pierre Dumas and the assisting nurse arrived, starting CPR and putting him in a portable oxygen mask.

He was 1,300 metres from the top of Mont Ventoux, within sight of its TV mast. It was five more minutes of pedalling away. Further down the field, Lewis and Hoban were first to come across their lifeless leader. They were apprehended by Alec Taylor, who urged them to carry on: the team was down to four men and he didn't want to lose anyone else. Hoban's thoughts, recounted in his autobiography *Watching the Wheels Go Round*, were: "'These things happen at the Tour, riders get completely smashed and simply jack it in. I expect we'll get the full explanation tonight back at the hotel.'" His blasé first impressions suggest that it was not out-of-the-ordinary for Simpson or other Tour riders to ride themselves to exhaustion. Meanwhile, Vin Denson had punctured at the foot of the climb and was among the backmarkers. "As I pushed through the crowd, Tom was getting the oxygen mask. I thought 'it looks like he's coming round a bit.' I kept thinking you stupid bastard, all this money we've lost, just thinking he'd done something stupid, not believing he was in such a bad state", Denson says.

"I was thinking 'the whole scheme was to get you on the rostrum [in the top three], that was the idea.' I'd been talking to him for days before saying 'forget the Tour, you're lying seventh. It's better to go for the Worlds, you've had a lot of bad luck.' And he wouldn't, he was determined he'd get on the rostrum. So he pushed himself too far."

Tom Simpson was taken by helicopter to Sainte-Marthe d'Avignon hospital and never regained consciousness. He was pronounced dead at 5.40pm.

The cycling world seemed to stop on its axis at the moment Simpson's death was announced. This was the sport's JFK moment; every person I ask remembers where they were when they heard the news. His old Tour room-mate Henri Duez was giving a lesson at his fledgling driving school

Stage 14 starts with a minute's silence, Carpentras, 1967 Tour de France

in northern France. When he heard the news on the radio, his legs turned to jelly. At home in Yorkshire, Billy Holmes switched on the TV and, seeing his old Olympic team-mate's photograph, he instinctively thought Simpson had taken the yellow jersey. When he heard the radio report, André Desvages was reminded of a premonition: he had dreamed of Simpson's death the previous night.

Then there was Tom's wife Helen, holidaying in Corsica. Sat on Pianottoli beach, her kids were playing under the Corsican sun, when the transistor radio reported news that Simpson had crashed. Her worry deepened when another bulletin hinted about its gravity. Leaving her two children with her mother, she went with her friend Blanche Leulliot to the nearby café in the village to telephone the Tour headquarters. Leulliot got through, heard the tragic update and took Helen back to their holiday home. There, she told Helen's father, who broke the news and accompanied her to Marseille and on to Avignon the next day. There, she saw Simpson's body in the morgue. "It was horrible", she says of that day, with a sharp intake of breath. The unimaginable had happened. Amid this grief, she was comforted by an iconic French singer. "Dalida was staying at the same hotel in Avignon. She sat on the end of my bed for a good two and a half hours, just talking, saying all the trauma she went through, because she'd actually tried to commit suicide [five months earlier]. Just being there, it was really nice [of her]."

Helen had lost the love of her life and the father of her children; the Tour peloton was without a popular, genial champion, British cycling was deprived of its figurehead and the British cyclists on Tour had lost a great friend and leader. Vin Denson remembers Harry Hall telling him that evening in Carpentras: "It took a long time

Bas Maliepaard and Felice Gimondi weep in Carpentras

A crowd of over 5,000 mourners turned out in Harworth for Simpson's funeral, 1967

before it registered. Hardly anybody ate. Hardly anybody spoke. It was a terrible evening. He was like a brother to me and suddenly, he's gone. That was such a shock." It was only the second fatality to take place on the Tour de France, after the Spaniard Francisco Cepeda, who crashed on a mountain descent in 1935.

The following day, at the start of the 14th stage, it was as if the life had been ripped from the race. The crowd in Carpentras were quiet and many riders wept. "It was the worst page of my life", says Jan Janssen. "I didn't want to continue. The solution was to go home. I'd lost a comrade, a friend." The remaining British quartet donned makeshift black armbands and a minute's silence was observed. In homage to Simpson, the bunch's *eminences grises* decided there would be no racing that day and that a British rider should win. Barry Hoban crossed the line first though, even today, there is still considerable contention with Vin Denson over which man was stipulated to take the victory.

By then, rumours had already been circulated about a connection between Simpson's death and doping. In the preliminary examination of his body at Avignon hospital, three small tubes were found in his jersey pockets by Dr Dumas, and were passed to the head officer of the Tour's *gendarme* unit. Two were empty, one contained two kinds of banned stimulant: Stenamina and Tonedron. Dumas, who had already felt the pill-boxes in Simpson's jersey pockets while attempting to resuscitate him, refused permission for burial. "The proof is very important for us. We need to find the reason for a young sportsman to die at that age", he told interviewer Maurice Seveno on French television programme *Panorama* the next day. His decision paved the way for the autopsy, a judicial inquiry and the unravelling of Simpson's complicated legacy.

On August 3, his autopsy results were released, confirming the rumours. Traces of amphetamine and methyl-amphetamine were found in Simpson's bloodstream, urine and intestines. The cause of

Helen watches from the doorway of Tom's parents' house before the funeral service at All Saints Parish Church

death was "cardiac collapse, which may be attributable to exhaustion, in which unfavourable weather conditions, an excessive workload and the use of medicines of the type discovered may have played a part." It was ruled that Simpson was not killed by the drugs – the dose alone was insufficient to do so – but they had contributed to his death. As a result of them, he "exceeded the limit of his physical capacity and brought on other conditions which caused his collapse."

This was the final hurricane wind in the perfect storm of his iconic death. One of the sport's great, handsome champions had died in the world's biggest cycling race, on its most feared, idiosyncratic mountain at the cusp of the TV revolution, with stimulants in his system. Simpson's status and the prominence of his death finally stripped away the wilful ignorance over doping and its dangers. With mortality waved in everyone's faces, nobody – not racers, the sport's governing body, the press, nor the public – could pretend it was a trifling matter anymore. Strangely, the judicial inquiry into the

death was closed four weeks after his autopsy: nobody had a case to answer. But Simpson has been answering it for the last 50 years.

Over the years, the presence of drugs in his system on Ventoux has become the headline of his life story. "We forget the fact that he had an infection. We forget that it was 45°C. We forget the fact that he was dehydrated chronically, and there was a culture [in cycling] of dehydration and low energy intake. Basically, what we see here is a perfect storm for a hyperthermic death", Dr Greg Whyte concludes.

Simpson was a cheat among many. But as the sport began a messy excoriation of doping, he was made the scapegoat of cycling's complicit corporation. Dead on the Ventoux at 29 years old, Tom Simpson simultaneously became frozen as a great cycling champion and its arch martyr.

"They made an example of Tom", his old Peugeot team-mate Emile Daems says. "But if he died from taking amphetamines on Mont Ventoux, then everyone should have died there."

A wreath of carnations and roses was sent by Tour de France riders to the funeral

208

BIRD ON THE WIRE

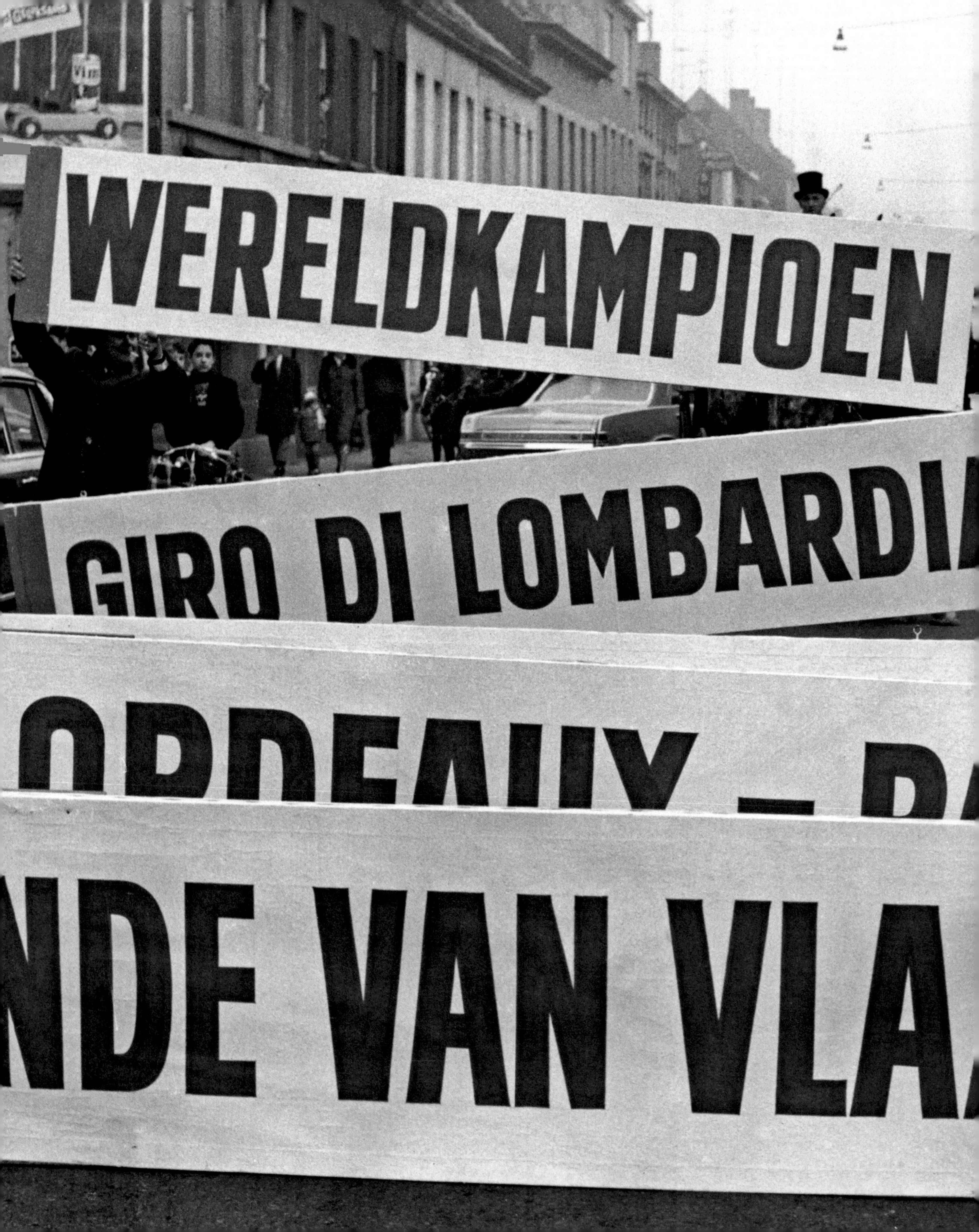
WERELDKAMPIOEN
GIRO DI LOMBARDI
NDE VAN VLA

"Like a bird on a wire, I have tried in my way to be free"

Leonard Cohen

Joanne Simpson places a red plastic box labelled "Ventoux stuff" on her dining room table and removes its contents. She brandishes one of several different-shaped rocks, which bears the marker pen message in Flemish: "I was here on my fourteenth birthday." There is a Navy beret, a Rapha casquette, an urn and flags from Wales, the Isle of Man and a Union Jack with Merci Mister Tom written on it.

Since his death, Simpson has become an icon and his granite memorial on Ventoux the locus of his remembrance. Tourists often stop on the way up or down the mountain to pay homage to the man and his sport at this monument, paid for by donations to *Cycling* in the months after his death. These are just a few of the thousands of mementos left there, ones that Joanne deemed too precious to go in the bin. Her father Tom Simpson has had an influence on a great many people. He has spawned other memorials in Harworth and Ghent, bike races and bike rides, jerseys, books, coffee mugs, documentaries, radio shows, films, a fund, an eponymous cycling magazine – and fostered great debate. Simpson's legacy is as complicated and multi-dimensional as the man himself.

His younger daughter is his next of kin yet, like the vast majority who pause at his shrine, she didn't know him. Four years old when he died, Joanne's only memory of "Daddy" is a man drinking milk straight from the bottle out of the fridge, which she knew to be naughty.

Her image of her father has been a 50-year emotional collage, added to by photographs, memorabilia and stories from family, friends, journalists and Simpson's former team-mates. As we sit drinking coffee in her living room in Destelbergen on the outskirts of Ghent one Sunday morning, next to a painting of Simpson and Eddy Merckx, I ask Joanne how it makes her feel that her father is still a fondly remembered cycling icon. To my surprise, she starts to cry. "I don't usually do this, sorry. He makes me happy when I think about him", she says, drying her eyes. "I'm so upset that I never knew him. When I hear stories, it makes me so angry – God, he must have been a nice guy, he must have been a lovely father, he always made lots of jokes."

Despite his absence, her mother Helen and stepfather Barry have remarked how similar their characters and looks sometimes are. Joanne

Simpson has also channelled the spirit of her father on the bicycle. In 1996, she heard over the radio that the Ghent-based classical singer Helmut Lotti was planning on cycling up the Ventoux with his wife. If they could do it, then why not her? She intentionally set 13 July 1997 as the date, 30 years since her father's death, and got training.

"Me, Mum and Barry had an argument the night before; they didn't want me to go up because the Ventoux was a no-no mountain for us, the Simpsons", she says. "It was an awful situation, but having the character of my dad, [it was like] 'I trained for this a whole year, there's nobody going to stop me now.' I wanted to finish those 1,300 metres that my dad was never able to do. I passed the monument, got to the top, came back and I think Mum and I cried in each other's arms for about half an hour."

Joanne with her father at home in Ghent, 1965

The Simpson memorial has a visual power to go with its emotional impact. From the exposed rocks there, the green plains of Provence spread out in a patchwork. It wouldn't have been the same to die at the foot of Ventoux, let alone in some charmless industrial village in northern France. "I cycle up and I think 'why? Why did you die there?' It's hard", Joanne says. "And then I stand at his monument and think 'you had the most beautiful place to die.'"

Every five years, she rides up Ventoux. "I love going there, it keeps me fit and close to him", she says. In the summer of 2016, Joanne helped to organise the refurbishment of the steps from the road to the memorial. The process showed the residual fondness still held for Simpson in his adopted home country. A Flemish stone company and contractor footed most of the bill themselves, helped by the Simpson Memorial Fund, while sealant experts Soudal provided the adhesive to ensure the granite steps could endure Ventoux's foulest weather.

Owing to the company's co-sponsorship of leading Belgian professional cycling team Lotto, cyclist Thomas De Gendt got involved too. Two months after his 2016 Tour de France stage win near the top of Ventoux, De Gendt drove 1,000 kilometres from his home in Flanders and spent a day riding up the mountain, filming a promotional video for Soudal and laying the first step on the way to the memorial. Simpson, the astute publicity hunter, would probably have smiled at De Gendt's motives. "I want to make sure that our sponsors were always happy, that's why I did the video", De Gendt, who lives locally to Joanne Simpson, says. "I've already been in a team [Vacansoleil] where the backer said they wanted to stop because they were not really happy with how the sponsorship was going. It was also nice to do for the symbolic meaning of the monument. I knew about Simpson, that he was world champion and the rest, but maybe younger riders from my age only get to see the images the media shows the most, and that's the Mont Ventoux tragedy. Maybe it's fair to say that they forget some of his victories."

Joanne Simpson is well aware of his polarised posthumous perception. Alongside the thousands of touching trinkets left up high on Ventoux, she has also seen a man drive past and spit in disgust at the memorial. To some, Simpson is a hero, a champion and a victim; to others, a villain, a cheat, part of the problem. For Simpson's younger daughter, the idea of her father as a doper is a subjective truth. The definitive answer lies in the result of his autopsy. Released three weeks after his death and widely reported on, the original file was thought to be buried deep in the Avignon judicial system. Joanne Simpson went to great lengths to find it in late 2016; really, it is remarkable that her family did not seek out the evidence sooner. Inquiries by her lawyer were met by responses from the Avignon hospital and Carpentras prosecutor that the medical files and archives from that period had been destroyed. Nevertheless, Simpson still holds out hope for one person out there with an original copy. "I just want the truth. I have no problem with it", she says. "When I'm there and see something special ... " She trails off, her eyes moistening again. "I don't know what I'll do with the information. But then we'll know." Is she a little afraid to find out? "No. It will hopefully give me and my mum peace of mind."

t would have been nice if Tom Simpson's death served as a wake-up call which provoked necessary soul-searching, changed methods from riders and the introduction of stringent measures from the sport's governing body. But this is professional cycling, not some schmaltzy Hollywood ending; the sport can often be more cruel or puzzling than it is beautiful. Its askew moral compass wasn't going to joltingly correct itself after decades of wonkiness. Colin Lewis alleges that the day after Simpson's death, as the grief-stricken peloton stood on the start line in Carpentras, he saw amphetamine pills in the jersey seam of French star Jean Stablinski. A week later, following the pivotal Puy-de-Dôme stage, Tour de France runner-up Julio Jimenez admitted: "I took stimulants, but everyone did like me. It was the last chance to try and take the yellow jersey from Pingeon ... everyone gulps down pills. We are all guilty in the same way."

At its annual congress in November 1967, the sport's governing body, the UCI, introduced a small, but significant anti-doping ruling: a one-month suspension for the first offence, extending to a life ban for the fourth. However, the rigour of the tests was dubious, as they had been before Simpson's death. Felice Gimondi tested positive at the 1968 Giro, but his month ban was overturned after doctors showed that the medication he claimed to have taken triggered an identical test result as if he had used amphetamines. In mid-July, Jacques Anquetil flaunted a one-month ban for missing a test by racing on the very day it was supposed to begin; his sanction was curtailed a week later because it appeared he had not been notified of the original anti-doping control.

Nevertheless, on the eve of the 1968 Tour, Jacques Goddet wrote in *L'Equipe*: "Dear Tom Simpson, you will not have fallen in vain on the stony desert of the Ventoux." The race was billed as the Tour de Santé – the Tour of Health. It was 300 kilometres shorter in total distance than the previous edition, and there were anti-doping tests after every stage. Their results would be turned around within 48 hours, enabling an immediate imposition of sanctions. Drinks were available from team cars to combat any claims of contaminated water bottles and, as a by-product, could help to prevent excessive dehydration. *L'Equipe* called the race "a turning point in the fight against doping"; in truth, it was a fly-catcher swat at a rampaging beast.

During the Tour, French racers Jean Stablinski and José Samyn both tested positive for the amphetamine corydrane, which was also the favoured pick-me-up of philosopher Jean-Paul Sartre. They were fined and given bans. Meanwhile, in a scene chillingly similar to that of Tom Simpson the previous year, Frenchman Jean Jourden collapsed in 40-degree heat after climbing the Col du Tourmalet. He abandoned the race; the verdict was sunstroke.

The Giant of Provence

Celebrating taking the yellow jersey with cravatte-wearing Ferdi Kübler and team mate Rolf Wolfshohl in Saint-Gaudens after stage 12, 1962 Tour de France

There was no clean bill of health for the so-called "Tour de Santé", or a Damascene conversion for cycling. As has been explored in previous chapters, the culture of looking for gains – fair, foul or pharmaceutical – has been embedded in society since the dawn of sport. The popular moral outcry and greater realisation of the problem that Simpson's death brought only served to make riders go to greater lengths to conceal their cheating, rather than stopping the cheating itself. Doping went underground, not away. Over time, the drugs became more potent and their use and administration were managed more closely, by qualified doctors and scientists. The favoured poison of the peloton changed from the comparatively primitive amphetamines to steroids, corticoids, human growth hormone and the blood booster erythropoietin (EPO) in the 1990s. The penalties for offences became stricter with ponderous slowness too. In the 1977 Tour, pre-race favourite Joop Zoetemelk tested positive for a banned stimulant after winning the time-trial up Avoriaz. He received the slap on the wrist of a 10-minute penalty and a £250 fine, still going on to finish ninth overall.

Little changed because of Simpson's death; arguably, the cheating intensified and got smarter. The Festina Affair of 1998, Operation Puerto in 2006 and the fall of Lance Armstrong are all landmark modern cycling scandals which show a fundamental lack of lessons learned and a culture barely altered. While stage distances and the need for riders to make money from an exhausting criterium circuit have decreased, base motivations and human nature have not changed. There is more money at stake and the self-same ferocious ambition of the top

A natural race leader, comfortable with all the attention that it brings, 1962 Paris-Nice

sportsman. "I wanted so badly to win the Tour this year", the favourite Alex Zülle said in 1999, after admitting why he used human growth hormone. Professional sport, governing bodies and anti-doping governance will seemingly always be fighting an under-resourced, rear-guard action against banned substance use. Perhaps it is the ongoing war on performance-enhancing drugs that helps to keep Simpson in the popular consciousness too.

A Tour de France visit to Mont Ventoux is always special because of the mountain's aura, its influence on the fight for the yellow jersey and the many notorious events that take place on the road to its bald summit. Every time the race returns, it is a form of both remembrance for Tom Simpson and a reminder of how he died with drugs in his system. His crime has a whopping half-life that risks burying memories of the buccaneering manner and ground-breaking victories on which his original fame was built.

Professional cycling is a peculiar sport, in which there are no hard and fast rules when it comes to the reception of perceived cheats. Some transgressions are swept under the carpet: the prolific Eddy Merckx remains feted, despite three doping positives; for others, it becomes their inescapable, defining action. It probably helped in the Sixties and Seventies that the internet and social media weren't around to spread the news and stoke outrage. Appearance, nationality, likeability and character come into the equation too. "A lot of bike riders aren't nice people", says one interviewee. "Tom was a good guy."

Simpson is at fault too; it was his own decision to cheat. But to dismiss him as a villain denies the engrained culture, the lack of tests for most of his career and the difficult decision that every rider in that era felt that they faced – take drugs, or be cheated out of results and a living. Nowadays, we criticise with stringent modern sensibilities an era in which anti-doping was a lax, fresh concept. The corrosive culture, the feckless governing body, the Tour de France and Simpson's entourage are also partly at fault. Maybe it's easier to blame an absent man than those faceless institutions.

The result of Simpson's autopsy was a condemning final word. The amphetamine and methamphetamine found in his system were empirical evidence of his cheating. It is reasonable to state there were other contenders with stimulants in their bloodstream that day or on later stages, which went undetected; men who still live today, with a fraction of the baggage attached to the Briton. Even those who test positive are given a chance for rehabilitation; in death, Simpson never had that. He seems to be doing eternal time for his crime.

On the other hand, his premature death led to his veneration. As Sir Bradley Wiggins writes in the foreword, Simpson has become a celestial and romanticised figure for millions who never knew him. There are parallels to be drawn between him and the likes of Ayrton Senna, James Dean, Kurt Cobain and Jimi Hendrix, who also died at similar ages. They are broadly connected by genius in their respective fields, good looks, panache, popularity and an endurance of their achievements. For all of them, life's arc was stopped at its peak. There were no straight-to-DVD films for Dean, no dodgy experimental albums for Cobain, no bad races for Simpson. They are frozen in time as young, great and beautiful.

For some observers, there may even be a morbid admiration of Simpson's death for its transcendence of limits. "Sport is destructive when it demands that athletes lose all sense of perspective in their pursuit of glory", anti-doping policy expert Paul Dimeo writes in *Drug Use in Sport*. "But in

life, in art, in music, in science, in philosophy, it is always those who lose their sense of perspective that make a lasting impact on the world."

The longevity of Simpson's fame is also partly down to the empathetic nature of road cycling. By and large, the sport's most prestigious races and hallowed places have not altered since the Briton's era. The casual enthusiast can ride up Mont Ventoux and, if so desired, get very close to feeling what history's great racers felt there. Few other sports have an ability to transcend time and place to give such a visceral connection. Cycling has a profound storytelling tradition too, be it sustained by café stop raconteurs, literature or internet forums. Simpson's unprecedented success, madcap character and audacious tactics have caught the attention of generations of British cyclists. Whatever you think of his drug-taking, his premature death sealed his immortality. This folk hero's tale is lodged deep in the soul of the domestic sport.

"When I was first learning about cycling and immersing myself in it as a kid, his name obviously came up", says Charly Wegelius, a British professional cyclist from 2000 to 2011. "If you remove the Foreign Legion generation from the Peugeot/ACBB days [which included Sean Yates, Robert Millar, Graham Jones and Paul Sherwen], he was the striking, stand-alone example for an aspiring rider from Britain that you could be successful in Europe. That story was really compelling."

As a budding teenage racer in the mid-Nineties, York-bred Wegelius was taken to see Simpson's grave in Harworth by his mentor, Russ Wake. "I guess it's because he thought that at some stage soon afterwards, I might be going to Europe to race my bike. I think that says a lot about how people think of Simpson and how important he is for people in British cycling", Wegelius says.

Until the glory years of Cavendish, Wiggins and Froome, Simpson had no equal in his home country for the quality of his wins. His was a very hard act to follow. In his absence, British racing on the Continent regressed; there was individual excellence from Barry Hoban, Robert Millar and Chris Boardman, but no concerted push as a nation. Who knows whether Simpson himself might have galvanised British cycling in a coaching or managerial role had he still been around?

The significant increase in the depth of British racers abroad is a recent development, and it owes much to the realisation of several of Simpson's dreams. On the back of National Lottery funding and an Olympic gold rush during the Noughties, cycling is no longer the modest Cinderella sport he knew, but a national juggernaut with hundreds of thousands of participants. In Team Sky, there is a British-backed road squad providing a pathway to the Continent for a core of British racers too. Crucially, it aims to offer a zero-tolerance policy on doping as an alternative to the culture of widespread cheating which Simpson and other British riders encountered during the 20th century.

Even with change over time, modern racers have come to empathise with some of Simpson's experiences. Charly Wegelius turned professional in 2000 and moved to Italy, encountering a Continental racing scene, in which survival required the few British outsiders to learn foreign languages and assimilate into the culture.

"I can remember seeing interviews of him where his English was starting to take on that clumsiness you get when you don't talk with English-speaking people for a long time. Those sort of things happened to me, to a degree, in the early years of my career", Wegelius says. "Generally, I'd say I identified with him a lot and admired his achievements a lot. He was a mythical symbol for me."

It has become traditional for British racers to remember Simpson when the Tour de France goes up Mont Ventoux, one of its sacred places. Wegelius's first time racing to its summit was on the penultimate stage of the 2009 Tour de France. For several kilometres near the top, he was worried he'd missed the memorial. "When I saw it, I knew that was it. It coincides with the moment in the race where things go a little bit quiet. Because

Photographed by Bernard Thompson waiting for the start of the Corona Grand Prix at London's Crystal Palace circuit as the junior race passes, 1964

the bottom part of the climb is so loud and the fans are so close – as Chris Froome will tell you. There's almost immediately fewer of them when you leave the forest."

Not a man who readily submits to shows of symbolism or patriotism, Wegelius tossed his water bottle towards it as he cycled past. "I surprised myself a bit that I felt the need to make some kind of gesture. Maybe it goes back to that day that I visited his grave." This kinship was shared by his compatriots: David Millar threw a casquette inscribed with the words "Tommy Simpson, RIP", and Mark Cavendish respectfully took his helmet off.

Wegelius has been through the sport's whole cycle, from being a dreaming teenager in Yorkshire to an ambitious young pro, world-weary domestique and his current role as a directeur sportif. He implicitly understands the hardships of the milieu and how it can blinker one's priorities. "Riding past his memorial and seeing that he died for that sport – he gave his life for it, essentially – was a heavy moment for me … it made me think 'is this the sport for me, that I'm giving so much of and that I cared so much about?' Because when you're really deep into it, it does feel a bit like life and death if you get dropped, sick or don't get selected for a race. People say 'it's only a bike race.' And it is only a bike race. I think cyclists, or top sportspeople in general, forget that very easily because they live in such a tunnel."

"When you race at that level, you put so much of your life into cycling, and it means so much to you. I think being faced so closely with the mortality, the ultimate price that he paid, brings home to you, on the one hand, how dangerous it can be. And on the other hand, the fact that it doesn't need to be as important as you feel it is. It feels sad for him that his career was so closely linked to the reasons of his death, but it's part of his story, isn't it?"

Six minutes ahead of Wegelius in Ventoux's lunarscape that day, Bradley Wiggins secured fourth place overall in the 2009 Tour de France, which equalled Great Britain's best ever performance at the time. That day, Wiggins cycled with a photograph of Simpson on his top tube. "As I began the climb, it felt as if his spirit was riding with me. It started on the early slopes and I imagined how Tom must have been feeling, riding towards his death, and the feeling grew as I climbed", he told the *Guardian*, adding later: "It was like a reason not to give up. I felt like I was doing it more for his memory than anything."

The race was Wiggins's breakthrough as a Grand Tour contender and the beginning of the end of what Simpson had set into motion with his day in the *maillot jaune* in 1962. Fifty years on, Wiggins rode down the Champs-Elysees as Britain's first winner of the Tour de France – on a British team. There are many comparisons to be drawn between Wiggins and Simpson, from the passing facial resemblance and Hour record obsessions to their deep Ghent connection. At the base of it all is character – they both stand out as charismatic, sometimes-controversial men who, love 'em or hate 'em, have flair and individuality. And ultimately, the public connects with sporting champions on deeper, emotional levels, not solely on the quantity or quality of their achievements.

When those that remember Simpson are gone, these handed-down stories will be his legacy, as will, hopefully, that memorial on Mont Ventoux. Yet, his memory shouldn't be restricted to that lunarscape as a sad sporting morality tale. He was a man with so much life; Simpson the pioneer, Simpson the entertainer, Simpson the risk-taker, Simpson the gentleman and Simpson the attacker ought to endure.

Cycling is a wonderful vehicle for freedom, and that's what Simpson was often driving at. He was the kid riding himself off the bike to exhaustion on the roads of Yorkshire, the rebellious adventurer going across to the European mainland and riding 200 kilometres in the lead to win the Tour of Lombardy, the attacker in unexpected places and the dreamer who wanted to live on a train. He frequently wanted to escape; in a poignant way, he did. Simpson may not have gone where he intended to go, but he has ended up where he needed to be.

Portrait of a champion, Herne Hill, 1963

221

Credits

Many thanks to everyone at Rapha especially to Daniel Blumire, who may well still be stuck on train somewhere near Maidenhead. Andy and Rob, my ex-team mates, did a fine job as ever. Thanks to Charlotte Croft and Sarah Skipper at Bloomsbury who always manage to spot something amiss and to the image handling talents of Linda Duong and Eoin Houlihan who polished the pictures to perfection. To all the photography agencies and in particular to Mark Leech at Welloffside, Fabrice Leboulanger at Pressesports, Toby Hopkins at Getty, Gareth Peers and Claire Hindson at the Press Association and Efe Mandrides at Time inc. Also to Rod Gunn for his scanning of Maurice Hart's wonderful collection. Lastly many thanks to Giada Moschetta and Jonathan Bortolazzi at EBS for their expert advice and patience.

As ever we cycling fans owe the photographers themselves a huge debt of thanks. Those agency professionals that worked during Tom's era had a insight and feel for the sport that is noticeably lacking these days. They perfectly captured the beauty of the sport with crude equipment and in conditions that were less than favourable, notably; Roger Viollet, Georges Menager, Jean Tesseyre, Gerry Cranham, John Otway, Len Thorpe, Ken Evans, Yvan Clench and Ian Clook.

Guy Andrews

Pressesports: outside back cover and 8, 13, 14, 15, 16, 17, 19, 20, 22, 23, 24, 29, 52, 54, 56, 58, 59, 62, 65, 70, 75, 84, 92, 94, 95, 99, 103, 107, 108, 111, 113, 115, 117, 118, 119, 120, 121, 122, 123, 128, 129, 131, 132, 137, 141, 142, 151, 159, 160, 162, 180, 190, 191, 193, 196, 199, 200, 212, 217, 219.

Time inc. Cycling Weekly archive: 21, 33, 34, 35, 45, 46, 55, 57, 61, 64, 66, 67, 77, 78, 81, 105, 126, 130, 133, 134, 136, 147, 154, 155, 156, 164, 167, 172, 176, 177, 185, 205, 207, 210.

Welloffside: 87, 88, 91, 97, 98, 104, 139, 140, 148, 150, 152, 153, 164, 171, 175, 178, 179, 181, 195, 202, 203, 220.

Getty Images: 42, 73, 74, 100, 112, 114, 182, 188, 215.

Also; Joe Thomas: 7, Glenn Steward: 26, Maurice Hart: 36, 37, 38, 39, 41, 49, PA Images: 204 and Bernard Thomson: 216.

Bibliography

While I went out of my way to find rare or untold stories for *Bird on the Wire*, the considerable existing literature around Simpson, Sixties cycling and the Tour de France proved particularly helpful as guides to the man and the era. This is by no means an exhaustive list, but merely some of the key texts and resources which helped me during the process.

Cycling Is My Life, Tom Simpson, Pelham, 1965
Put Me Back On My Bike, William Fotheringham, Yellow Jersey Press, 2002
Le Tour de France, Pierre Chany, Librarie Plon, 1972
Continental Cycle Racing, Noel Henderson, Pelham Books, 1970
White Heat: A History of Britain in the Swinging Sixties, Dominic Sandbrook, Little Brown, 2006
A History of Drug Use in Sport 1876–1976, Paul Dimeo, Routledge, 2007
French Cycling: A Social and Cultural History, Hugh Dauncey, Liverpool University Press, 2012
The Eagle of the Canavese, Herbie Sykes, Mousehold Press, 2008
Mr. Tom, Chris Sidwells, Mousehold Press, 2000
Brian Robinson: Pioneer, Graeme Fife, Mousehold Press, 2010
The Eagle of Toledo, Alasdair Fotheringham, Aurum Press, 2012
I Was There, Daily Telegraph and Sunday Telegraph writers, Collins, 1967

Written media
Cycling, L'Equipe, Sporting Cyclist, Doncaster Gazette, La Stampa, The Daily Telegraph, Miroir Sprint, But et Club and Miroir des Sports

Online resources
Bikeraceinfo.com, Dewielersite.net, Memoire-du-cyclisme.eu and Ina.fr

Films
Something To Aim At by Ray Pascoe
The World of Tommy Simpson by Ray Pascoe and produced by BBC Films

Thanks

This book couldn't have been done without a supporting cast of cycling luminaries from the Fifties and Sixties. It was a pleasure and a privilege to accompany them down memory lane and I'm grateful for such generosity with their time, warm hospitality and insightful anecdotes. Cycling might be bigger now, but it's still one big family – with some cracking characters.

Special thanks to the Hoban/Simpson family for their openness and conviviality, Rapha, Simon Mottram and Sir Bradley Wiggins, plus Simon Richardson and Cycling Weekly for generous use of their archives. The Bibliothèque nationale de France, Doncaster Central Library and the British Library – which felt like a second home at times – were also invaluable for research and resources.

Thanks to editor Guy Andrews and Rob Johnston, Rouleur's art director, for their invaluable work in the conception, design and editing of this book; it's come a long way since that gin and tonic at the Dean Street Townhouse.

Thanks to Anya Hayes for copy editing, Oskar Scarsbrook for transcription, *miglior fabbro* Edward Pickering for advice, Lucy and Sophie for sisterly support, Herbie Sykes, Bruce Sandell, Ian Cleverly, the Rouleur team and, in no particular order, Norman Hill, Christian Perichon, Dr. Greg Whyte, Ken Hartley, Pete Graham, Neville and Sarah Veale, Jean Dumont, Alf Howling, Arne Houtekier, Margaret Hedley, Isabel Best, Raymond Kerckhoffs, Ray Pascoe, Mike Breckon, Ernie Riley, Pascal Sergent, "Monsieur" James Startt, Marco Pastonesi, Bédoin Tourism Office, Edmond Hood, Barry Hoban for his expert car manoeuvring (sorry again for backing into your wall), Brian Robinson for sharing contacts and Maurice Hart for his cracking, unseen photographs.

Warmest regards to Peter Hibberd, "Captain" Chris Phillips, Jolyon Beales, Bill Showler, Adam Wilkinson and the York crew for dragging me away from the grindstone and keeping my spirits high.

Last and certainly not least, my heartfelt thanks to Josie for her love, support, patience and putting up with a partner who spent more time with Tom Simpson than her for months on end.

Andy McGrath, Author

Andy McGrath is a London-based cycling journalist and the managing editor of Rouleur Magazine. He has worked at Cycling Weekly and Cycle Sport, and written for The Guardian, The Financial Times and others. He co-authored the Official Treasures of the Tour de France and edited the Rouleur publication "Merckx: The Greatest".

When Tom Simpson came over to London in February for the Corona press lunch, he said his immediate goal was Milan. Here he is at the moment of victory in the great Italian race with Poulidor well beaten.

Above: Eighteen years ago, Fausto Coppi wins the same race after an historic lone break. Finishing point is the same—but the addition of Poggio hill means that the riders now appear from the other direction on Via Roma.

Some road stars find it difficult to adapt themselves to the speed and atmosphere of an indoor track. Not so Tom Simpson, who was already an accomplished performer on the path before taking up road work. Here is Tom in the Brussels six-day race handling his partner, Freddy Eugen, of Denmark.

THE SPORT OF KINGS OF THE ROAD & TRACK

Based at St. Gervais for the cyclists' winter sports championships, they were able to see the nearby Sallanches circuit. But, as these pictures show, winter sports were favourite!

It was in February that I met Tom Simpson for the first time this year. Nice was a lovely place to be, and in the warm sunshine everything looked gay—especially the riders who were giving a last touch to their bikes before the start of the Grand Prix de Nice, one of the first "real" races of the season. There can be few workers who are more pleased when their holidays are over than professional cyclists!

The organisers on the Côte d'Azur are lucky. The best men are nearly all there and willing to start in races, no matter what the prize list is. They know only too well that they could hardly find their best form if they did not make serious efforts at this time of the year.

So Tom Simpson was there, Bobet, and Altig and dozens of other big names of continental cycling, ready to sweat on the hills of the colourful Côte d'Azur.

Tom was in a café filling his bidons with mineral water. At once it was obvious the Yorkshire boy was in really good health, that he had been very careful about his diet and had not put on much weight during the winter. He was in a happy mood, but nevertheless he talked seriously.

"You see, René, I realise that last year I made a number of mistakes I could have avoided. But I admit I was, sometimes, a bit lost and did not know exactly how to manage. So many people around me were giving different advice. If only I had known as much then as I do now," he said.

Tom was being rather critical with himself, I thought. In an extremely short time he had built himself a name which really means something to any French, Belgian or Italian

CYCLING and Mo

SIMPSON
Wins Bordeaux — Paris, greatest of the Continental road race classics

BURTON
Breaks 'Hour Barrier'

BONNER